Leon Tolstoy

Voltaire

*The Wit & Wisdom of*

# *Great Writers*

First Published in Great Britain in 2006 by
House of Raven Book Services
King's Sutton
OX17 3RS

Typeset in Mylius Sans and ITC Officina Serif
Design, illustration and photography: David Coventon

Printed in China by Imago


ISBN: 1905403070

*The Wit & Wisdom of*

# *Great Writers*

*Compiled and Edited by Nick Holt*

Anybody can m
history. Only a
man can write

Oscar Wilde

H. James

P. G. Wodehouse

Voltaire

Henry D. Thoreau

Jane Austen

Leon Tolstoy

P. G. Wo

Voltaire

# CONTENTS

There are over 1,200 quotes in this collection. Each quote that appears is numbered (i.e. ·123). These numbers run sequentially throughout the book. Use the index at the back to find Great writers or publications from which these quotes come. The index is listed in alphabetical order by surname.

*To all of them.*
*May they live on when*
*txt msgng is gone*

BOOKS DO FURNISH A ROOM

*Every age hath its book.*

**The Koran,** *Chapter 13* ·1

# Books

*Of making many books there is no end; and much study is a weariness of the flesh.*

**Bible,** *Ecclesiastes 12:12* ·2

*He hath not fed of the dainties that are bred in a book; he hath not eat paper, as it were; he hath not drunk ink.*

**William Shakespeare,**
*Love's Labours Lost IV.ii (1595)* ·4

*The English public takes no interest in a work of art until it is told that the work in question is immoral.*

**Oscar Wilde** ·6

*The generall end therefore of all the booke is to fashion a gentleman or noble person in vertuous and gentle discipline.*

**Edmund Spenser,** *The Faerie Queene (1596)* ·3

*Some books are to be tasted, others to be swallowed, and some few to be chewed and digested; that is, some books are to be read only in parts; others to be read but not curiously; and some few to be read wholly, and with diligence and attention. Some books also may be read by deputy, and extracts made of them by others.*

**Francis Bacon,** *Essays 'Of Studies' (1625)* ·5

*Reformers are always finally neglected, while the memoirs of the frivolous will always be eagerly read.*

Henry 'Chips' Channon, *Diary, 7 July 1936* •7

*No place affords a more striking conviciton of the vanity of human hopes, than a pubic library.*

Samuel Johnson, in *The Rambler*
*23 March 1751* •8

*Provided that nothing like useful knowledge could be gained from them, provided they were all story and no reflection, she had never any objection to books at all.*

Jane Austen, *Northanger Abbey* •9

*Books are good enough in their own way, but they are a mighty bloodless substitute for life.*

Robert Louis Stevenson,
*Virginibus Puerisque*
*'An Apology for Idlers'*
*(1881)* •10

*The novel is not likely to die. There is no substitute, at least so far, that can handle psychological complexity and inwardness and reflection in the way that the novel can.*

Julian Barnes, in *Paris Review Winter 2000-2001* •11

*Every novel is a story, but life isn't one. More of a sprawl of incidents.*

Doris Lessing, *Under My Skin (1994)* •12

*Yes – oh dear, yes – the novel tells a story.*

E.M. Forster, *Aspects of the Novel (1927)* •13

*A great library contains the diary of the human race.*

George Dawson, speech on opening Birmingham Free Library, *26 October 1866* •14

*Yes, the collection of a lifetime and I guard it well. I never lend! Only fools lend books. All the books on this shelf once belonged to fools.*

Anonymous, quoted to Bertrand Russell in C. Williams-Ellis, *Architect Errant (1971)* •15

*It is a mistake to think that books have come to stay. The human race did without them for thousands of years and may decide to do without them again.*

E.M. Forster, *attrib.* •16

*Speak of the moderns without contempt, and of the ancients without idolatry.*

Lord Chesterfield, *Letters to his Son (1774)* •18

*All books are divisible into two classes: the books of the hour and the books of all time.*

John Ruskin, *Sesame and Lillies (1865)* •17

*Art is much older than democracy, and art is uncompromisingly elitist.*

Robertson Davies, *lecture, Yale 20 February 1990* •19

*Books will speak plain when counsellors blanch.*

Francis Bacon, *'Of Counsel' (1625)* •20

*A book is a mirror; if an ass peers into it, you can't expect an apostle to look out.*

Georg C Lichtenberg ·21

*Wealth and power are much more likely to be the result of breeding than they are of reading.*

Fran Lebowitz, *Social Studies (1981)* ·22

*It is wonderful that even today, with all the competition of radio, television, films, and records, the book has kept its precious character. A book is somehow sacred. A dictator can kill and maim people, can sink to any kind of tyranny, and only be hated. But when books are burnt the ultimate tyranny has happened. This we cannot forgive.*

John Steinbeck, *attrib.* ·23

*In his library he had always been sure of leisure and tranquillity; and though prepared… to meet with folly and conceit in every other room in the house, he was used to be free from them there.*

Jane Austen, *Pride and Prejudice (1813)* ·24

*Being a librarian doesn't help. I've always found them close relatives of the walking dead.*

Alan Bennett, in *Anthony Thwaite, Larkin at Sixty (1982)* ·25

*When a man writes a letter to himself, it is a pity to post it to somebody else. Perhaps the same is true of a book.*

D.H. Lawrence, *Aaron's Rod (1922)* •26

*If an army of monkeys were strumming on typewriters they might write all the books in the British Museum.*

Sir Arthur Eddington, English astronomer, physicist and mathematician; *The Nature of the Physical World (1928)* •27

*Publishing a book is often very much like being put on trial, for some offence which is quite other than the one you know in your heart you've committed.*

Margaret Atwood, *Negotiating with the Dead: A Writer on Writing (2002)* •28

*The multitude of books is a great evil. There is no measure or limit to this fever of writing; everyone must be an author; some out of vanity to acquire celebrity; others for the sake of lucre or gain.* Martin Luther, *Table-Talk (1569)* •29

*I'm replacing some of the timber used up by my books. Books are just trees with squiggles on them.*

Hammond Innes on growing trees; interview in *Radio Times 18 August 1984* •30

*I hate books; they only teach us to talk about things we know nothing about.*

Jean-Jacques Rousseau, *Émile (1762)* ·31

*A book is a fragile creature. It suffers the wears of time, it fears rodents, the elements, clumsy hands.* Umberto Eco ·34

*Books do furnish a room.*

Anthony Powell, title of a novel *(1971)* ·32

*The Librarian was, of course, very much in favour of reading in general, but readers in particular got on his nerves…He liked people who loved and respected books, and the best way to do that, in the Librarian's opinion, was to leave them on the shelves where nature intended them to be.* Terry Pratchett, *Men at Arms (1993)* ·35

*Child! Do not throw this book about; Refrain from the unholy pleasure Of cutting all the pictures out! Preserve it as your chiefest treasure.*

Hilaire Belloc, dedication in *A Bad Child's Book of Beasts (1896)* ·33

*Let your bookcases and your shelves be your gardens and your pleasure-grounds. Pluck the fruit that grows therein, gather roses, the spices and the myrrh.*

Medieval Jewish philosopher Judah Ibn Tibbon, in Israel Abrahams, *Jewish Life in the Middle Ages* ·36

*Stories are like genes. They keep part of us alive after the end of our story.*

A.S. Byatt, *On Histories and Stories (2000)* ·39

*A room without books is as a body without a soul.* Cicero ·37

*When an old man dies, a library burns down.*

African proverb. ·38

*For me, endings are never really endings. They're just there for the sake of the book.*

Carol Shields, interview in *Observer, 28 April 2002* ·40

¶

# Reading

There are many ways of educating our feelings, but I recommend reading as that which is most ready to hand.

**Robertson Davies,** *lecture, Yale 20 February 1990* •43

Take up and read, take up and read.

**St. Augustine,** *Confessions* •41

Reading a book is like rewriting it for yourself… You bring to… anything you read, all your experience of the world. You bring your history and you read it in your own terms.

**Angela Carter,** in *Marxism Today January 1985* •42

But who shall be the master? The writer or the reader?

**Denis Diderot,** *Jacques le Fataliste et son maitre (1796)* •44

As soon as I put a full stop on a book, it's not my thing any more. It ceases to be mine even more when the reader picks it up.

**Zadie Smith,** in *Observer 25 August 2002* •45

*One writes only half the book; the other half is with the reader.*

Joseph Conrad, *letter to Cunnighame Grahame, 1897* •46

*What is written without effort is in general read without pleasure.*

Samuel Johnson, in *William Seward, Biographia (1799)* •47

*The reading of good books is like a conversation with the best men of past centuries — in fact like a prepared conversation, in which they reveal only the best of their thoughts.*

René Descartes, *Le Discours de la méthode (1637)* •48

*If reading is your pleasure read, but don't expect the magic to flow from Willa Cather into you and the words to come right out of your bone marrow, pre-ordained, and arrange themselves powerfully, perfectly, in sentences and paragraphs. If you want to be a writer, write. Write something.*

Helen Gurley Brown, *The Writer's Rules (1998)* •49

*When I am dead, I hope it may be said, 'His sins were scarlet, but his books were read.'*

Hilaire Belloc, *'On His Books', 1923* •50

*Choose an author as you choose a friend.*

Wentworth Dillon, Lord Roscommon, *Essay on Translated Verse (1684)* •51

*Readers and writers are united in their need for solitude… in their reach inward, via print, for a way out of loneliness.*

Jonathan Franzen, *How to be Alone? 2002 'Why bother?'* •52

*As a reader, I want a book to kidnap me into its world. Its world must make my so-called real world seem flimsy. Its world must lure me to return. When I close the book, I should feel bereft.*

Erica Jong, in *The Writer's Handbook (1997)* •53

*A great book should leave you with many experiences, and slightly exhausted at the end. You live several lives while reading it.*

William Styron, in *Writers at Work, first series (1958)* •54

*If you read twenty or thirty pages by a writer, and want to continue, you are in his sea and swimming in that sea. He can write quite badly after that. Because by that time, you're in his sea, and you're moving forward.*

Brian Moore, Canadian novelist, in *Rosemary Harthill, Writers Revealed (1989)* •55

*People say that life is the thing, but I prefer reading.*

Logan Pearsall Smith, *Afterthoughts (1931) 'Myself'* •56

*Reeling and Writhing, of course, to begin with,' the Mock Turtle replied; 'and then the different branches of Arithmetic — Ambition, Distraction, Uglification, and Derision.'*

Lewis Carroll, *Alice's Adventures in Wonderland (1865)* •57

*The primary object of a student of literature is to be delighted. His duty is to enjoy himself: his efforts should be directed to developing his faculty of appreciation.*

Lord David Cecil, *Reading as one of the Fine Arts (1949)* ·58

*Everyone probably thinks that I'm a raving nymphomaniac, that I have an insatiable sexual appetite, when the truth is I'd rather read a book.*

Madonna, *Q Magazine 1991* ·59

*A man ought to read just as inclination leads him; for what he reads as a task will do him little good.*

Samuel Johnson, in *James Boswell, Life of Samuel Johnson (1791) 14 July 1763* ·60

*In science, read, by preference, the newest works; in literature, the oldest.*

Edward George Bulwer-Lytton, *Caxtoniana (1863) 'Hints on Mental Culture'* ·61

*I think you should only read those books which bite and sting you.*

Franz Kafka, *letter to Oskar Pollak, 1904* ·62

*I do not hesitate to read… all good books in translations. What is really best in any book is translatable — any real insight or broad human sentiment.*

Ralph Waldo Emerson, *Society and Solitude (1870) 'Books'* ·63

*Reading is to the mind what exercise is to the body.*

Richard Steele, in *The Tatler* *18 March 1710* •64

*Read not to contradict and confute, nor to believe and take for granted, nor to find talk and discourse, but to weigh and consider.* Francis Bacon, *Essays (1625) 'Of Studies'* •65

*There are two motives for reading a book; one, that you enjoy it; the other, that you can boast about it.*

Bertrand Russell, British philosopher •66

*We want incident, interest, action: to the devil with your philosophy.*

Robert Louis Stevenson, *letter to John Meiklejohn, February 1880* •67

*There are times when I think that the reading I have done in the past has had no effect except to cloud my mind and make me indecisive.*

Robertson Davies, Canadian journalist and novelist. •68

*Don't read too much now: the dude Who lets the girl down before The hero arrives, the chap Who's yellow and keeps the store, Seem far too familiar. Get stewed: Books are a load of crap.*

Philip Larkin, *'Study of Reading Habits' (1964)* •69

*Magazines all too frequently lead to books and should be regarded by the prudent as the heavy petting of literature.*

Fran Lebowitz, *Metropolitan Life, 1978* •70

*Books have to be read (worse luck it takes so long a time). It is the only way of discovering what they contain. A few savage tribes eat them, but reading is the only method of assimiliation revealed to the West.* E.M. Forster ·71

## Four Sorts of Readers

*1. Sponges that suck up everything and, when pressed give it out in the same state, only perhaps somewhat dirtier –. 2. Sand Glasses… whose reading is only a profitless measurement and dozing away of time –.*

*3. Straining Bags,who get rid of whatever is good and pure, and retain the dregs. 4. and lastly, the Great-Moguls' Diamond Sieves… who assuredly retain the good, while the superfluous or impure passes away and leaves no trace.*

Samuel Taylor Coleridge, *Notebook, 1806-1810* ·72

*Reading isn't an occupation we encourage among police officers. We try to keep paper work down to a minimum.* Joe Orton, *Loot (1967)* ·73

*The man who doesn't read good books has no advantage over the man who can't read them.*

Mark Twain ·74

*There are worse crimes than burning books. One of them is not reading them.*

Russian writer and exile Joseph Brodsky, *remark, 1991* ·75

*It's very, very easy not to be offended by a book. You just have to shut it.*

Salman Rushdie, in *Daily Telegraph* 8 October 1994 'They Said It' •76

¶

# *THE LITERARY ART*

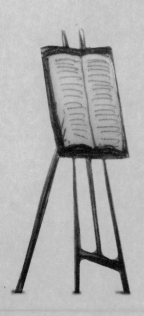

*The last thing one knows in constructing a work is what to put first.*

**Blaise Pascal,** *Pensées (1670)* ·77

The Art

*Art is meant to disturb, science reassures.*

Georges Braque, *Le Jour et la nuit: Cahiers 1917-52* •80

*The acceptance that all that is solid has melted into air, that reality and morality are not givens but imperfect human constructs, is the point from which fiction begins.*

Salman Rushdie, *'Is Nothing Sacred?' (Herbert Read Memorial Lecture) 6 February 1990* •78

*Life being all inclusion and confusion, and art being all discrimination and selection.*

Henry James, preface to *The Spoils of Poynton (1909 ed.)* •79

*Story-telling is an instinct to come to terms with mystery, chaos, mess.*

Graham Swift, in *Clare Boylan (ed.) The Agony and the Ego (1993)* •81

*Writing is play in the same way that playing the piano is 'play', or putting on a theatrical 'play' is play. Just because something's fun doesn't mean it isn't serious.*

Margaret Atwood, in an interview, *November 1989, Earl G. Ingersoll (ed.) (1990)* •82

*To invoke in oneself a feeling one has experienced and having evoked it in oneself then by means of movements, lines, colours, sounds, or forms expressed in words, so to transmit that feeling – this is the activity of art.*

Leo Tolstoy, *What is Art? (1898)* •83

*Journalism encourages haste… and haste is the enemy of art.*

Jeanette Winterson, *Art Objects (1995)* •84

*True ease in writing comes from art, not chance,*

*As those move easiest who have learned to dance.*

Alexander Pope, *An Essay on Criticism (1711)* •85

*You can't produce art by trying, setting up exacting standards, by talking about critical minutiae, by the Flaubert method. It is produced with great ease, in an almost off-hand manner, and without self-consciousness.*

Raymond Chandler, *letter to Jamie Hamilton, 17 June 1949* •86

*I like to feel that a writer is perfectly cool and detached, regarding other people's feelings or his own, like a God who has got beyond them.*

T.S. Eliot, *letter 19 September 1917* •87

*I cannot imagine how it must feel for an author to see someone else's interpretation of their own inner vision. I am constantly amazed at how appreciative most of them manage to be.*

Shirley Hughes on illustration, *A Life Drawing (2002)* •88

*What we ask a theory for, is to give us back an old subject illuminated by a new light in order to realize that only from that point of view the object can be really understood.*

Umberto Eco, in *Drama Review March 1977* •89

*A writer wastes nothing.*

F. Scott Fitzgerald, in Sheilah Graham and Gerald Frank, *Beloved Infidel (1959)* •90

*One sentence. Two at most. If you can't tell yourself what your story is in one or two sentences, you're already running into trouble. Even in Moby Dick, it comes down to Captain Ahab chases a whale and doesn't get it.*

Gerald Petievich, in *The Writer's Digest Handbook of Novel Writing (1992)* •91

*To write well, express yourself like the common people, but think like a wise man.*

Aristotle •92

*Art requires, above all things, a suppression of one's self.*

Henry James, *Mr Walt Whitman (1865)* •93

*Anyone could write a novel given six weeks, pen, paper and no telephone or wife.*

Evelyn Waugh •94

*The act of writing is a kind of guerilla warfare; there is no vacation, no leave, no relief. In actuality there is very little chance of victory. You are, you fear… likely to be defeated by your own fondest dreams.*

Walter Mosley, in *Writers on Writing: Collected Essays from the New York Times (2001)* •95

*I believe that all those painters and writers who leave their wives have an idea at the back of their minds that their painting or writing will be the better for it, whereas they only go from bad to worse.*

Patrick White, *letter to Barry Humphries, 7 October 1973* •96

*The true genius is a mind of large general powers, accidently determined to some particular direction.*

Samuel Johnson, *Lives of the English Poets (1779-81)* •97

*The only time a human being is free is when he or she makes a work of art.*

Friedrich von Schiller, in *Edmund White The Burning Library (1994)* •98

*Drama is life with the dull bits left out.*

Alfred Hitchcock, *attrib.* •99

*Books choose their authors; the act of creation is not entirely a rational and conscious one.*

Salman Rushdie, in *The Independent 4 February 1990* •100

*Even the slightest thing contains a little that is unknown. We must find it. To describe a blazing fire or a tree in a plain, we must remain before that fire or tree until they no longer resemble for us any other tree or any other fire. That is the way to become original.*

Gustave Flaubert advising Guy de Maupassant; recalled by de Maupassant in *Preface, Pierre et Jean (1888)* •101

*Nothing has yet been said that's not been said before.*

Terence, *Eunuchu* •102

¶

# Inspiration

*For a start, I've got to be out of my head to write.*

Shane MacGowan of The Pogues *(1989)* •103

*To turn events into ideas is the function of literature.*

George Santayana, *attrib.* •104

*It came from mine own heart.*
  *So to my head*
*And thence into my fingers*
  *it tricklèd;*
*Then to my pen, from whence*
  *immediately*
*On paper I did dribble*
  *it daintily.*

John Bunyan, *The Holy War '
Advice to the Reader'(1682)* •105

*But words come halting forth, wanting*
  *Invention's stay;*
*Invention, Nature's child, fled step-dame*
  *Study's blows…*
*Biting my truant pen, beating myself*
  *for spite,*
*'Fool,' said my Muse to me; 'look in*
  *thy heart and write.'*

Philip Sidney, *Astrophil and Stella,
Sonnet 1 (1591)* •106

*All writers know that on some golden mornings they are touched by the wand — are on intimate terms with poetry and cosmic truth. I have experienced these moments myself. Their lesson is simple: It's a total illusion. And the danger in the illusion is that you will wait for those moments.*

J.K. Galbraith •107

*The process of writing… consists of sitting in one place for several hours every day and groaning immoderately while you make marks of one colour on a surface of another. Inspiration has precious little to do with it and brutal toil a great deal.*

Richard Ford, in *Writer's on Writing: Collecting Essays from The New York Times (2001)*•108

*I don't know anything about inspiration because I don't know what inspiration is — I've heard about it, but I never saw it.*

William Faulkner, interview in *Paris Review, Spring 1956* •109

*The childhoods of writers are thought to have something to do with their vocation, but when you look at these childhoods they are in fact very different. What they often contain, however, are books and solitude.*

Margaret Atwood, *Negotiating with the Dead: A Writer on Writing (2002)* •110

*Write while the heat is in you… The writer who postpones the recording of his thoughts uses an iron which has cooled to burn a hole with. He cannot inflame the minds of his audience.*

Henry David Thoreau, *letter, 1 February 1852* •111

*If you are in difficulties with a book, try the element of surprise: attack it at an hour when it isn't expecting it.*

H.G. Wells •112

*The pen is the tongue of the mind.*

Miguel de Cervantes •113

*Unfortunately for novelists, real life is getting way too funny and far-fetched. It's especially true in Miami, where the daily news seems to be scripted by David Lynch. Fact is routinely more fantastic than fiction.*

Carl Hiaasen, in *Writers on Writing: Collected Essays from the New York Times* •115

*What do you think of the world? You, the prism, measure the light of the world; it burns through your mind to throw a different spectroscopic reading onto white paper than anyone else anywhere can throw.*

Ray Bradbury, *Zen in the Art of Writing (1990)*•114

*He has gained every point who has mixed profit with pleasure, by delighting the reader at the same time as instructing him.*

Horace, *Ars Poetica* •116

*Think before you speak is criticism's motto; speak before you think creation's.*

E.M. Forster, *Two Cheers for Democracy (1951)* •117

*The more indignant I make the bourgeois, the happier I am.*

Gustave Flaubert, *letter, 25 July 1842* ·118

*Each year brings new problems of Form and Content, new foes to tug with: at Twenty I tried to vex my elders, past Sixty it's the young whom I hope to bother.*

W.H. Auden, *Shorts I* ·121

*There is a splinter of ice in the heart of a writer.*

Graham Greene, explaining why he was fascinated by witnessing the death of a child while he was in hospital recovering from appendicitis; in *A Sort of Life (1971)* ·119

*Asked why he wrote The Name of the Rose: "I felt like poisoning a monk."* Umberto Eco, in *George Plimpton (ed.) The Writer's Chapbook (1989)* ·122

*When starting to think about any novel, part of the motive is: I'm going to show them, this time. Without that, a lot of what passes under the name of creative energy would be lost.*

Kingsley Amis, in *George Greenfield, Scribblers for Bread (1989)* ·120

*I draw from life —
but I always pulp my
acquaintance before
serving them up. You
would never recognize
a pig in a sausage.*

Frances 'Fanny' Trollope, English novelist,
in *S. Baring-Gould, Early Reminiscences
1834-1864 (1923). Remark made c.1848* •123

*Why does my Muse only speak
    when she is unhappy?*
*She does not, I only listen when I
    am unhappy*
*When I am happy I live and
    despise writing*
*For my Muse this cannot but
    be dispiriting.*

Stevie Smith, *My Muse (1964)* •124

*It's easier to write about
things that are falling
apart than things that
are beautiful and perfect.*

Beck, American Singer/Songwriter *(1996)*•125

*Tragedy is thus a representation
of an action that is worth
serious attention, complete in
itself and of some amplitude…
by means of pity and fear
bringing about the purgation
of such emotions.*

Aristotle, *Poetics* •126

The composition of a tragedy requires testicles.

Voltaire, on being asked why no woman had ever written 'a tolerable tragedy'; *letter to Byron from John Murray, 2 April 1817* •127

The original writer is not he who refrains from imitating others, but he who can be imitated by none.

François-René Chateaubriand, *Le Génie du Christianisme (1802)* •130

In every first novel the hero is the author as Christ or as Faust.

Oscar Wilde, *attrib.* •128

Unless the almighty maker them ordain

His dark materials to create more worlds

John Milton, *Paradise Lost (1667)* •131

Show me a hero and I will write you a tragedy.

F. Scott Fitzgerald, *The Crack-Up (1936)* •129

*One of the disabling weaknesses of current Western literature is its unwillingness or inability to engage with the dance of the spirit in the sciences. Music and the arts are equipped to do better.*

George Steiner, *'A Festival Overture' (Edinburgh University Festival Lecture, August 1996* •132

*No story comes from nowhere; new stories are born from old — it is the new combinations that make them new.*

Salman Rushdie, *Haroun and the Sea of Stories (1990)* •133

¶

# Style

An author arrives at a good style when his language performs what is required of it without shyness. Cyril Connolly, *Enemies of Promise (1938)* •136

The web, then, or the pattern; a web at once sensuous and logical, an elegant and pregnant texture: that is style, that is the foundation of the art of literature. Robert Louis Stevenson, *The Art of Writing (1905) 'On some technical Elements of Style in Literature' (written 1885)* •134

Proper words in proper places, make the true definition of a style. Jonathan Swift, *Letter to a Young Gentleman lately entered into Holy Orders 9 January 1720* •137

I know of only one rule: style cannot be too clear, too simple. Stendhal, *letter to Balzac, 30 October 1840* •135

Prose is architecture, not interior decoration, and the Baroque is over. Ernest Hemingway, in *Jeffrey Meyers, Hemingway (1985)* •138

*Good prose is like a window-pane.*

George Orwell, *Collected Essays vol.1
'Why I Write' (1968)* •139

*Every author of some value
transgresses against 'good
style', and in that transgression
lies the originality (and hence
the raison d'être) of his art.*

Milan Kundera, *Testaments Betrayed (1995)* •140

*The only obligation
to which in advance
we may hold a novel,
without incurring the
accusation of being
arbitrary, is that
it be interesting.*

Henry James,
*The Art of Fiction (1888)* •141

*To find a form that
accommodates the
mess, that is the task
of the artist now.*

An ever optimistic Samuel Beckett,
*Proust (1961)* •142

*A writer must be as objective as a
chemist: he must abandon the subjective;
he must know that dung-heap play a
very reasonable part in landscape, and
that evil passions are as inherent in
life as good ones.* Anton Chekhov,
*letter to M.V. Kiselev,
14 January 1887* •143

*There is no such thing as a
moral or immoral book. Books
are well written, or badly written.*

Oscar Wilde, *The Picture of Dorian Gray (1891)* •144

*What a book a devil's chaplain might write on the clumsy, wasteful, blundering, low, and horridly cruel works of nature!*

**Charles Darwin**, *letter to J.D. Hooker, 13 July 1856* •145

*Oh! It is only a novel!... only Cecilia, or Camilla, or Belinda: or, in short, only some work in which the most thorough knowledge of human nature, the happiest delineation of its varieties, the liveliest effusions of wit and humour are conveyed to the world in the best chosen language.*

**Jane Austen**, *Northanger Abbey (1818)* •146

*Style and structure are the essence of a book; great ideas are hogwash.*

**Vladimir Nabokov**, *in George Plimpton (ed.), Writers at Work (4th series, 1977)* •147

*The structure of a play is always the story of how the birds came home to roost.*

**Arthur Miller**, *in Harper's Magazine August 1958* •148

*The famous rules, which the French call Des Trois Unitez, or the Three Unities, which ought to be observed in every regular play; namely, of Time, Place, and Action.*

**John Dryden**, *A Essay of Dramatic Poesy (1668)* •149

*Grasp the subject,
the words will follow.*

Cato the Elder ·150

*There is nothing to write about,
you say. Well then, write and let
me know just this – that there is
nothing to write about; or tell me in
the good old style if you are well.*

Pliny the Younger, *Letters* ·151

*The writer's problem is, how
to strike the balance between
the uncommon and the ordinary
so as on the one hand to give
interest, and on the other to
give reality.* Thomas Hardy,
notebook July 1881 ·152

*The province of literature is a
debatable line. It lies on the confines
of two distinct territories. It is under
the jurisdiction of two hostile powers;
and like other districts similarly
situated it is ill-defined, ill-cultivated,
and ill-regulated. Instead of being
equally shared between its two rulers,
the Reason and the Imagination, it
falls alternately under the sole and
absolute dominion of each. It is
sometimes fiction. It is sometimes theory.*

Lord Macaulay, *History (1828)* ·153

*Having to read footnotes
resembles having to go
downstairs to answer the
door while in the midst of
making love.*

Noël Coward ·154

*It is sometimes necessary to repeat what we all know. All mapmakers should place the Mississippi in the same location, and avoid originality.*

Saul Bellow, *Mr Sammler's Planet (1970)* •155

*In nearly all good fiction, the basic — all but inescapable — plot form is: A central character wants something, goes after it despite opposition (perhaps including his own doubts), and so arrives at a win, lose, or draw.*

John Gardner, *On Becoming a Novelist (1983)* •156

*Where shall I begin, please your Majesty?' he asked. 'Begin at the beginning,' the King said gravely, 'and go on till you come to the end: then stop.'*

Lewis Carroll, *Alice's Adventures in Wonderland (1865)* •157

# My way is to begin with the beginning.

Lord Byron, *Don Juan (1819-24)* •158

*The king died and then the queen died', is a story. 'The king died and then the queen died of grief' is a plot.*

E.M. Forster, *Aspects of the Novel (1927)* •159

*Sir, Perhaps the lack of literary inventiveness in modern opening lines is due to the effect of the word processor. When I ran the first line of Moby Dick through my spell-checker, it suggested changing this to 'Call me Fishmeal'.*

Helen Grayson, *letter to The Times 18 October 1997* •160

*When I sit down to write a novel
I do not at all know, and I do not
very much care, how it is to end.*

Anthony Trollope, *Autobiography (1883)* •161

*The beginning of a book holds
more apprehensions for the
novelist than the ending. After
living with a book for a year or
two, he has to come to terms
with his unconsciousness —
the end will be imposed. But if
a book is started in the wrong
way, it may never be finished.*

Graham Greene, *In Search of a Character
(1961)* •162

*It has always seemed to me
as unnatural for two people
to write a book together as
for three people to have a
baby.* Evelyn Waugh is suspicious of
literary collaboration, *letter,
30 July 1962* •163

*Great things of course
have been done by solitary
workers; but they have
usually been done with
double the pains they
would have if they had
been produced in more
genial circumstances.*

Henry James, *Hawthorne (1879)* •164

*A sequel is an
admission that
you've been reduced
to imitating yourself.*

Don Marquis, US writer •165

*With each book you write you should lose the admirers you gained with the previous one.*

André Gide, in *Edmund White, The Burning Library (1994)* •166

*I am of the opinion that the reader each writer wants is part and parcel of the novel's conception. His special presence is evoked in the style and texture of each line. What we call style is the explicit inclusion of some readers in, and all other readers out.*

Wright Morris, in *Afterwords: Novelists on Their Novels (1969)* •167

*When you're a novelist, you're writing a play but you're acting all the parts, you're controlling the lights and the scenery and the whole business, and it's your show.* Robertson Davies, in *Paris Review 1989* •168

*Journalism is about working yourself up into a lather over things you previously felt nothing about. It is diametrically opposed to what you do as a novelist, which is very slowly to discover what it is you really think about things.*

Kazuo Ishiguro, in *Guardian 15 May 1996* •169

*The chief difference between good writing and better writing may be measured by the number of imperceptible hesitations the reader experiences as he goes along. The author functions as a kind of forest guide. Does our reader trip over unfamiliar words…stub his toe on an ambiguous antecedent?*

James J. Kilpatrick, *The Writer's Art (1984)* •170

*A good novel tells us the truth about its hero; but a bad novel tells us the truth about its author.*

G.K. Chesterton, *Heretics (1905)* ·171

*The most important advice I would suggest to beginning writers: Try to leave out the parts that readers skip.*

Elmore Leonard, in *Snoopy's Guide to the Writing Life (2002)* ·172

*There is a magical quality in names. To change the name is to change the character.*

Graham Greene, *Ways of Escape (1980)*·173

*My theory of writing I can sum up in one sentence. An author ought to write for youth in his own generation, the critics of the next, and the schoolmasters of ever after.*

F. Scott Fitzgerald, *letter to the Booksellers' Convention, April 1920* ·174

*Only two classes of books are of universal appeal. The very best and the very worst.* Ford Madox Ford, *Joseph Conrad (1924)* ·175

*What the American public always wants is a tragedy with a happy ending.*

William Dean Howells explains to Edith Wharton why her play *The House of Mirth* wouldn't run on Broadway. *October 1906,* in *R.W.B. Lewis, Edith Wharton (1975)* •176

¶

# WRITERS

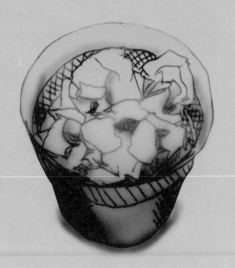

But those who cannot write,
  and those who can,

All rhyme, and scrawl, and scribble,
  to a man.

**Alexander Pope,** *Imitations of Horace (1737)* ·177

# On Writing

The only end of writing is to enable the readers better to enjoy life, or better to endure it.

Samuel Johnson, *A Free Enquiry (1757)* •180

So all my best is dressing
  old words new,

Spending again what is
  already spent.

William Shakespeare, *Sonnet 76* •178

Read over your compositions, and where ever you meet with a passage which you think is particularly fine, strike it out.

Samuel Johnson, quoting a college tutor,
*James Boswell, Life of Samuel Johnson (1791)*
*30 April 1773* •181

Writing, Madam, is a mechanic part of wit; a gentleman should never go beyond a song or a billet.

Sir George Etheridge,
English Restoration dramatist;
*The Man of Mode (1676)* •179

Three or four families in a country village is the very thing to work on.

Jane Austen, *letter to Anna Austen,*
*9 September 1814* •182

*A person who can write a long letter, with ease, cannot write ill.* Jane Austen, Miss Bingley in *Pride & Prejudice* •183

*People don't deserve to have good writing, they are so pleased with bad.*

Ralph Waldo Emerson, *Journals 1841* •185

*Remove at least fifty superlatives in each chapter. Never say 'Oliver's burning passion for Helen.' The poor novelist has to make us believe in the burning passion without ever naming it: that would be immodest.*

Stendhal, *letter to Mme Gaulthier, 4 May 1834* •18

*The hero of my tale — whom I love with all the power of my soul, whom I have tried to portray in all his beauty, who has been, and is, and will be beautiful — is Truth.*

Leo Tolstoy, *Sevastopol in May (1855)* •186

*Since when was genius found respectable?*

Elizabeth Barrett Browning, *Aurora Leigh (1857)* •187

*But a man or woman who publishes writings inevitably assumes the office of teacher or influences the public mind… He can no more escape the moral taste, and with it the action of the intelligence, than a setter of fashion in furniture and dress can fill the shops with his designs and leave the garniture of persons and houses unaffected by his industry.*

George Eliot, *attrib.* •188

*No man would have dared to write and publish such books... no man could have written such delineations of female passion... No! They are women, who by their writings have been doing the work of the enemy of souls... Women... who might have been bright and shining lights in their generation.* Francis E. Paget, *Lucretia (1868)* •189

*Genius does what it must, and Talent does what it can.*

Owen Meredith, *Last Words of a Sensitive Second-Rate Poet (1868)* •190

*Persons attempting to find a motive in this narrative will be prosecuted; persons attempting to find a moral in it will be banished; persons attempting to find a plot in it will be shot.*

Mark Twain, *The Adventures of Huckleberry Finn (1884)* •191

*If there is anything said in two sentences that could have been as clearly and as engagingly said in one, then it's amateur work.*

Robert Louis Stevenson, *letter to William Archer, February 1888* •192

*One should never make one's debut with a scandal. One should reserve that to give an interest to one's old age.*

Oscar Wilde, *The Picture of Dorian Gray, (1891)* •193

*As to the Adjective: when in doubt, strike it out.* Mark Twain, *Pudd'nhead Wilson (1894)* •194

*It is wonderful how much news there is when people write every other day; if they wait for a month, there is nothing that seems worth telling.*

O. Douglas, *Penny Plain (1920)* •197

*Enduring fame is promised only to those writers who can offer to successive generations a substance constantly renewed; for every generation arrives upon the scene with its own particular hunger.* André Gide, *Pretexts (1903)* •195

*An average English word is four letters and a half. By hard, honest labour I've dug all the large words out of my vocabulary and shaved them down till the average is three and a half letters… I never write metropolis for seven cents because I can get the same money for city. I never write policeman, because I can get the same money for Cop.*

Mark Twain, *Mark Twain's Speeches (1923)* •198

*Omit needless words… A sentence should contain no unnecessary words, a paragraph no unnecessary sentences, for the same reason that a drawing should have no unnecessary lines and a machine no unnecessary parts.*

William Strunk, *The Elements of Style (1918)* •196

*To my daughter Leonora without whose never-failing sympathy and encouragement this book would have been finished in half the time.*

P.G. Wodehouse, dedication, *The Heart of a Goof (1926)* •199

*What no wife of a writer can ever understand is that a writer is working when he's staring out of the window.*

Burton Rascoe, American newspaper editor. •200

*A woman must have money and a room of her own if she is to write fiction.*

Virginia Woolf, *A Room of One's Own (1929)* •201

*The moment a man sets his thoughts down on paper, however secretly, he is in a sense writing for publication.*

Raymond Chandler, working notes on the Julia Wallace murder case, in *Raymond Chandler Speaking (1962)* •202

*We write to taste life twice, in the moment, and in retrospection... We write to be able to transcend our life, to reach beyond it. We write to teach ourselves to speak with others, to record our journey into the labyrinth.*

Anais Nin •203

*Literature is mostly about having sex and not much about having children. Life is the other way round.*

David Lodge, *The British Museum is Falling Down (1965)* •204

Beware of writing to me. I always answer… My father spent the last 20 years of his life writing letters. If someone thanked him for a present, he thanked them for thanking him and there was no end to the exchange but death. Novelist Evelyn Waugh, son of noted editor and publisher Arthur Waugh; letter to Lady Mosley, 30 March 1966 •205

There are three reasons for becoming a writer. The first is that you need the money; the second, that you have something to say that you think the world should know; and the third is that you can't think what to do with the long winter evenings.

Quentin Crisp, The Naked Civil Servant (1968) •206

The idea of being a writer attracts a good many shiftless people, those who are merely burdened with poetic feelings or afflicted with sensibility.

Flannery O'Connor, in Mystery and Mannes (1969) •207

*Ridicule is the only honourable weapon we have left.*

Muriel Spark, The Desegregation of Art (1971) •208

You shouldn't pay very much attention to anything writers say. They don't know why they do what they do. They're like good tennis players or good painters, who are just full of nonsense, pompous and embarrassing.

John Barth, in The Contemporary Writer (1972) •209

*Each writer is born with a repertory company in his head. Shakespeare has perhaps twenty players, and Tennessee Williams has about five, and Samuel Beckett one — and maybe a clone of that one. I have ten or so, and that's a lot. As you get older, you become more skilful at casting them.* Gore Vidal, in *Times Herald (Dallas) 18 June 1978* •210

*The writer must be universal in sympathy and an outcast by nature: only then can he see clearly.* Julian Barnes, *Flaubert's Parrot (1984)* •212

*If you can't annoy somebody, there's little point in writing.*

Kingsley Amis •213

*Everyone thinks that writers must know more about the inside of the human head, but that is wrong. They know less, that's why they write: trying to find out what everyone else takes for granted.*

Margaret Atwood, *Dancing Girls and Other Stories (1982)* •211

*If you want your writing to be taken seriously, don't marry and have kids, and above all, don't die. But if you do have to die, commit suicide. They approve of that.*

Ursula Le Guin, *Prospects for Women in Writing (1986); repr. Dancing at the Edge of the World (1989)* •214

*A writer's visible life and the root of imagination do not connect above ground.*

Mavis Gallant, *Paris Notebooks: Essays and Reviews (1986)* ·215

*Writers live twice. They go along with their regular life… But there's another part of them that they have been training. The one that lives everything a second time. That sits down and sees their life again and goes over it. Looks at the texture and the details.* Natalie Goldberg, *Writing Down the Bones (1986)* ·216

*Writing is like driving at night in the fog. You can only see as far as your headlights, but you can make the whole trip that way.*

US writer E.L. Doctorow, in *George Plimpton, Writers at Work (1988)* ·217

*I don't use a typewriter. It's too heavy, too much trouble. I use a notebook, and I write in my bed. Ninety-five percent of everything I've written has been done in bed.*

Paul Bowles, in *George Plimpton (ed.) The Writer's Chapbook (1989)* ·218

*My pen… is a Waterman's, black enamel with a trim of gold. When I write with it, I feel as if I'm wearing a perfectly tailored suit, and my hair is pulled back into a chignon.*

**Mary Gordon,** in *Writers on Writing: Collected Essays from The New York Times (2001)* •219

*In the mid-eighties I was a grateful convert to computers… I like the provisional nature of unprinted material held in the computer's memory — like an unspoken thought.*

**Ian McEwan,** in *Paris Review Summer 2002* •220

*If a writer writes truthfully out of individual experience then what is written inevitably speaks for other people. For thousands of years storytellers have taken for granted that their experiences must be general. It never occurred to them that it is possible to divorce oneself from life.*

**Doris Lessing,** in *Partisan Review, Fall 1992 (special issue) 'Unexamined Mental Attitudes Left Behind by Communism'.* •221

*All writers are thieves; theft is a necessary tool of the trade.*

**Nina Bawden,** *Mothers: Reflections by Daughters (1995)* •222

*Most novelists, knowing that ongoing work is fed by ongoing life, prize their telephones, their correspondence, and their daily rubbing up against family and friends.*

Carol Shields, *Jane Austen (2001)* •223

# *Writers, those professionals of dissatisfaction.*

Susan Sontag, in *Writers on Writing: Collected Essays from the New York Times (2001)* •224

*I love deadlines. I love the whooshing noise they make as they go by.*

Douglas Adams; in *Guardian 14 May 2001* •225

*The boundaries of science have expanded in recent decades in a rather interesting way. Emotion, consciousness, human nature itself, have become legitimate topics for the biological sciences. And these subjects of course are of central interest to the novelist. The invasion of our territory ought to be fruitful.* Ian McEwan, in *Paris Review Summer 2002* •226

*If I had to give young writers advice, I would say don't listen to writers talk about writing or themselves.*

Lillian Hellman, American playwright. •227

*That is one last thing to remember: Writers are always selling somebody out.*

Joan Didion, *Slouching Toward Bethlehem, preface (1968)* •228

¶

*When I was a little boy,*
*they called me a liar, but*
*now that I am grown up,*
*they call me a writer.*

Polish-born American writer Isaac
Bashevis Singer, in *Bibliophile*
*July 1986* •229

*Whoa, there's enough, whoa*
*now, little book! We have got*
*to the post! But you want to*
*go on further and keep going,*
*there's no holding you at the*
*final sheet, as though you had*
*not finished the business which*
*was finished even on page one.*

Martial, *Epigrammata* •230

*It could be said that in this book I have*
*only made up a bunch of other men's*
*flowers, providing of my own only the*
*string that ties them together.*
Montaigne, *Essais (1580)* •231

# I write of melancholy,
# by being busy to
# avoid melancholy.

Robert Burton, *The Anatomy of Melancholy*
*(1621-51) 'Democritus to the Reader'* •232

**On Themselves**

*I desire to set before my fellows the likeness of a man in all the truth of nature, and that man myself.* Jean-Jacques Rousseau, *Confessions (1782)* •233

*I am going to take a heroine whom no-one but myself will much like.* Jane Austen, on starting *Emma,* in *J.E. Austen-Leigh, A Memoir of Jane Austen (1926 ed.)* •236

*I think I may boast myself to be, with all possible vanity, the most unlearned and uninformed female who ever dared to be an authoress.* Jane Austen, *letter 11 December 1815* •234

*No, indeed, I am never too busy to think of S. And S. I can no more forget it than a mother can forget her suckling child.* Jane Austen, *letter to her sister, Cassandra* •235

*Between you and me, I am not deep, but I am very wide, and it takes time to walk around me.* Honoré de Balzac, *letter to Countess Maffei, 1837* •237

*To such critics I would say, To you I am neither man nor woman — I come before you as an author only.*

Charlotte Brontë, *letter to W.S. Williams, 16 August 1849* •238

*When I want to read a novel, I write one.*

Benjamin Disreali, in *W. Monypenny and G. Buckle, Life of Benjamin Disreali vol.6 (1920)* •239

*It is splendid to be a great writer, to put men into the frying pan of your words and make them pop like chesnuts.*

Gustave Flaubert, *letter 3 November 1851* •240

*I cannot write books handling the topics of the day; it is of no use trying. Nor can I write a book for its moral.*

Charlotte Brontë, *letter to George Smith, 30 October 1852* •241

*An author who talks about his own books is almost as bad as a mother who talks about her own children.*

Benjamin Disraeli •242

*I have many irons in the fire, and am bursting with writableness.*

Henry James, *letter 29 May 1878* ·243

*I wrote such melancholy things when I was young that I am obliged to be unusually cheerful and robust in my old age.*

Christina Rossetti, in *Jan Marsh, Christina Rossetti (1994)* ·244

*Medicine is my lawul wife and literature is my mistress. When I get tired of one I spend the night with the other.* Anton Chekhov, *letter to A.S. Suvorin, 11 September 1888* ·245

*When I face that fatal manuscript it seems to me that I have forgotten how to think — worse! how to write. It is as if something in my head had given way to let in a cold grey mist. I knock about in it till I am positively, physically sick.* Joseph Conrad, *letter, 5 August 1896* ·246

*I never accepted a knighthood because to be me is honour enough.*

George Bernard Shaw ·247

I can live for two months on a good compliment.

Mark Twain •248

The port from which I set out was, I think, that of the essential loneliness of my life.

Henry James, *letter, 2 October 1900* •249

After all, one knows one's weak points so well, that it's rather bewildering to have the critics overlook them and invent others.

Edith Wharton, *letter, 19 November 1909* •251

After my marriage, she edited everything I wrote. And what is more — she not only edited my works — she edited me! Mark Twain of his wife, Livy; in *Van Wyck Brooks, The Ordeal of Mark Twain (1920)* •250

I hate the sort of licence that English people give themselves... to spread over and flop and roll about. I feel as fastidious as though I wrote with acid.

Katherine Mansfield, *letter to John Middleton Murry, 19 May 1913* •252

*The business of selection and revision is simply hell for me — my efforts to cut out 50,000 words may sometimes result in my adding 75,000.*

American novelist Thomas Wolfe, *letter to Maxwell Perkins, his editor at Scribner's, 17 November 1928* •253

*My memory is certainly in my hands. I can remember things only if I have a pencil and I can write with it and play with it. I think your hand concentrates for you.* Rebecca West, in *George Plimpton (ed.) The Writer's Chapbook (1989)* •254

*It scarcely needs criticism to bring home to me that much of my work has been slovenly, haggard and irritated, most of it hurriedly and inadequately revised, and some of it as white and pasty in its texture as a starch-fed nun.*

H.G. Wells, *Experiment in Autobiography (1934)* •255

*I was driven into writing because I found it was the only way a lazy and ill-educated man could make a decent living. I am not complaining about the wages. They always seemed to me disproportionately high. What I mind so much is the work.* Evelyn Waugh, in *Nash's Pall Mall Magazine, March 1937* •256

*You know you're writing well when you're throwing good stuff into the wastebasket.*

Ernest Hemingway, *attrib.* •257

*I often covered more than a hundred sheets of paper with drafts, revisions, rewritings, ravings, doodlings, and intensely concentrated work to produce a single verse.*

Dylan Thomas, *letter, 25 May 1948* •258

*Better to write for yourself and have no public, than write for the public and have no self.*

Cyril Connolly, in *Pritchett (ed.), Turnstile One* •259

*If I had to choose between betraying my country and betraying my friend, I hope I should have the guts to betray my country.* Novelist E M Forster, *'What I Believe', in* Two Cheers for Democracy, *1951* •260

*I am a drinker with a writing problem.*

Brendan Behan •261

*From the time I was nine or ten, it was a toss-up whether I was going to be a writer or a painter, and I discovered by the time I was sixteen or seventeen that paints cost too much money, so I became a writer because you could be a writer with a pencil and a penny notebook.*

Irish novelist and short-story writer Frank O'Connor, in *George Plimpton (ed.) The Writer's Chapbook (1989)* •262

*I always start with a title…
and then work round different
meanings. A novel is, for me,
always an elaboration of
the title.* Muriel Spark; in *Scotsman 1962* •263

*The ideal reader of my novels is
a lapsed Catholic and a failed
musician, short-sighted, colour-blind,
auditorily biased, who has read the
books that I have read. He should
also be about my age.*

Anthony Burgess, in *George Plimpton (ed.),
Writers at Work 4th Series (1977)* •266

# *A doormat in a world of boots.*

A self-assessment from novelist and short-
story writer Jean Rhys; quoted in *Guardian
6 December 1990* •264

*I am the kind of writer
that people think other
people are reading.*

V.S. Naipaul, in *Radio Times 14 March 1979* •267

*The writer's abiding problem
is that he gets so sick of his
own company but daren't
take too long away from it.*

Peter Nichols, *Diary,
2 January 1973* •265

*I sometimes lose interest in the
characters and get much more
interested in the trees and animals.*

Toni Morrison, in *George Plimpton (ed.)
The Writer's Chapbook (1989)* •268

*Details fascinate me. I love to pile up details. They create an atmosphere.*

Muriel Spark, *Curriculum Vitae (1992)* •271

*It's probably a form of childish curiosity that keeps me going as a fiction writer. I... want to open everybody's bureau drawers and see what they keep in there. I'm nosy.*

Margaret Atwood, in an interview, *December 1986; in Earl G. Ingersoll (ed.) Margaret Atwood: Conversations (1990)* •269

*I'm not too keen on characters taking over; they do as they are damn well told.*

Iain Banks, in *Stan Nicholls (ed.) Wordsmiths of Wonder (1993)* •272

*I always think of my novels as being the lives of the characters.*

Patrick White, *Patrick White Speaks (1990)* •270

*When I read something saying I've not done anything as good as Catch-22 I'm tempted to reply, 'Who has?'*

Joseph Heller, in *The Times 9 June 1993* •273

*I need people's good opinion. This is something in myself I dislike because I even need the good opinion of people I don't admire. I am afraid of them. I am afraid of what they will say to me. I am afraid of their tongues and their indifference.*

Ruth Rendell, in *Anthony Clare, In the Psychiatrist's Chair II (1995)* •274

*Self-knowledge does not necessarily help a novelist. It helps a human being a great deal but novelists are often appalling human beings.*

Peter Carey •277

# *I am as shallow as a puddle.*

Helen Fielding, creator of *Bridget Jones* •275

*My writing is like fine wine; the more you read, the more you get from it. Reading it once is like taking a dog to the theatre.*

V.S. Naipaul, winner of the *Nobel Prize for Literature* •276

*For me it's therapy. Anything that's going on in my life, anything like that, I just give to Rebus as a plot. So I'm working through my worries through him.*

Ian Rankin, in *Observer 18 March 2001* •278

*I can do to him whatever I like. I'm allowed to torture him as much as I want. He's mine.*

J.K. Rowling defends her right to put *Harry Potter* through the mill ·279

*Slowly but surely the pen became mightier than the double-quick pick-up timestep with shuffle.*

Zadie Smith, on her shifting ambitions from dancer to author, in *Independent* *7 September 2002* ·281

*It felt as if some woman had come out of nowhere saying she was my daughter's mother.*

J.K. Rowling on being falsely accused of plagiarism; in *The Times 20 September 2002* ·280

*I write because I want more than one life; I insist on a wider selection. It's greed plain and simple. When my characters join the circus, I'm joining the circus. Although I'm happily married, I spent a great deal of time mentally living with incompatible husbands.*

Anne Tyler, Pulitzer Prize-winning American writer ·282

*What to do with all this talent, how to stay alive until I've gotten down to it. I still feel that.*

Saul Bellow to his biographer on 30 August 1992, in *New Yorker* *26 June 1995* •283

¶

# BOOKS ARE MORE THAN BOOKS

*A well-written Life is almost
as rare as a well-spent one.*

**Thomas Carlyle,** *Critical and Miscellaneous Essays
(1838) John Paul Friedrich Richter* ·284

*Nobody can write the life of a man, but those who have eat and drunk and lived in social intercourse with him.*

Samuel Johnson, in *James Boswell, Life of Samuel Johnson (1791) 31 March 1772* •285

*Biographies are likely either to be acts of worship or acts of destruction. And the best ones have elements of both.*

Biographer and childrens author Humphrey Carpenter, in conversation with Lyndall Gordon; in *John Batchelor (ed.), The Art of Literary Biography (1995)* •286

*Biographers know nothing about the intimate sex lives of their own wives, but they think they know all about Stendhal's or Faulkner's.*

Milan Kundera, *Testaments Betrayed (1995)* •287

*I read biographies backwards, beginning with the death. If that takes my fancy I go through the rest. Childhood seldom interests me at all.*

Alan Bennett, *Writing Home (1994)* •288

*Formerly we used to canonize our heroes. The modern method is to vulgarise them. Cheap editions of great books many be delightful, but cheap editions of great men are absolutely detestable.*

Oscar Wilde, *The True Function and Value of Critism, 1890.* •289

*Biography is in some ways the most brutish of all the arts. It shifts about uncomfortably in the strangely uncertain middle ground between deliberate assassination and helpless boot-licking.* Dennis Potter, in *The Times* 24 February 1968 •290

*Every great man nowadays has his disciples, and it is always Judas who writes the biography.*

Oscar Wilde, *Intentions (1891) The Critic as Artist* •291

*Anyone turning biographer commits himself to lies, to concealment, to hypocrisy, to flattery, and even to hiding his own lack of understanding, for biographical truth is not to be had, and even if it were it couldn't be used.*

Sigmund Freud, in a *letter to Arnold Zweig, who had suggested being his biographer.* •292

*Oh, fond attempt to give a deathless lot To names ignoble, born to be forgot!*

William Cowper, *On Observing Some Names of Little Note Recorded in the Biographia Britannica (1782)* •293

*I have decided to keep a full journal, in the hope that my life will perhaps seem more interesting when it is written down.*

Sue Townsends Adrian Mole, in *Adrian Mole: The Wildnerness Years (1993)* •294

*It's the good girls who keep the diaries. The bad girls never have the time.*

Tallulah Bankhead •295

*What is more dull than a discreet diary? One might just as well have a discreet soul.*

Henry Chips Channon, *Diary, 26 July 1935* •296

*I never travel without my diary. One should always have something sensational to read in the train.*

Oscar Wilde, *The Importance of Being Earnest (1895)* •297

*Autobiography is probably the most respectable form of lying.*

Humphrey Carpenter, *Patrick White Explains Himself,* in *The New York Times Book Review 7 February 1982* •298

*An Autobiography is an obituary in serial form with the last instalment missing.*

Quentin Crisp, *The Naked Civil Servant, 1968.* •299

*Theres no such thing as autobiography. There's only art and lies.*

Jeanette Winterson in *Guardian, 5 July 1994* •301

*Autobiographies tell more lies than all but the most self-indulgent fiction.*

A.S. Byatt, *Sugar (1988)* •300

*Only when one has lost all curiosity about the future has one reached the age to write an autobiography.*

Evelyn Waugh, *A Little Learning (1964)* •302

¶

I walk many times into the pleasant
fields of the Holy Scriptures, where
I pluck up the goodly green herbs of
sentences, eat them by reading, chew
them up musing, and lay them up at
length in the seat of memory… so I
may less perceive the bitterness of
this miserable life.

Elizabeth I, in *Adam Fox (ed.)*
*A Book of Devotions (1970)* •305

*The one essential part
of all my education.*

John Ruskin, of his daily Bible
readings with his mother; in
*Dictionary of National Biography.* •303

*You cannot name
any example in
any heathen author
but I will better it
in Scripture.*

James I, in *Thomas Overbury (1581-1613),*
*'Crumms Fal'n From King James's Table'*
*published 1715* •304

*Never forget, gentlemen,
never forget that this
is not the Bible. This,
gentlemen, is only a
translation of the Bible.*

Richard Whately to a meeting of his diocesan
clergy, as he held up a copy of the *'Authorized
Version'. In H. Solly, These Eighty Years (1893)* •306

*Translation it is that openeth the window, to let in the light; that breaketh the shell, that we may eat the kernel; that putteth aside the curtain, that we may look into the most holy place; that removeth the cover of the well, that we may come by the water.*

Bible, Authorized Version (1611) '
The Translators to the Reader' •307

*There's a Bible on that shelf there. But I keep it next to Voltaire — poison and antidote.*

Bertrand Russell, in Kenneth Harris Talking To
(1971) 'Bertrand Russell' •308

*I read the book of Job last night. I don't think God comes well out of it.*

Virginia Woolf, letter to Lady Robert Cecil,
12 November 1922 •309

¶

*Literature is the question minus the answer.*

Roland Barthes, in
*New York Times 1978* •310

*Classic. A book which people praise and don't read.*

Mark Twain, *Following the Equator*
*(1897)* •312

*Great literature is simply language charged with meaning to the utmost possible degree.*

Ezra Pound, *How To Read (1931)* •311

*A classic is something that everybody wants to read.*

Mark Twain, *The Disappearance of Literature,*
*1900* •313

*Definition of a classic: a book everyone is assumed to have read and often thinks they have.*

Alan Bennett, *Independent on Sunday, 1991* •314

*Literature is the art of writing something that will be read twice; journalism what will be read once.*

Cyril Connolly, *Enemies of Promise (1938)* •315

*The virtue of much literature is that it is dangerous and may do you extreme harm.*

John Mortimer, in *C.H. Rolph, Books in the Dock (1969)* •316

*You're familiar with the tragedies of antiquity, are you? The great homicidal classics?*

Tom Stoppard, *Rosencrantz and Guildenstern are Dead (1967)* •317

*A man with a belly full of the classics is an enemy of the human race.*

Henry Miller, *Tropic of Cancer, 1930* •318

*And now I have finished the work, which neither the wrath of Jove, nor fire, nor the sword, nor devouring age shall be able to destroy.*

Ovid, *Metamorphoses* ·319

*A classic is a book that has never finished saying what it has to say.*

Italo Calvino, *The Literature Machine (1987)* ·320

¶

*Literature is a luxury;*
*fiction is a necessity.*

**G.K. Chesterton,** *The Defendants (1901)*
*A Defence of Penny Dreadfuls* •321

*Fiction is to the grown man*
*what play is to the child;*
*it is there that he changes*
*the atmosphere and*
*tenor of his life.*

**Robert Louis Stevenson,**
*Memories and Portraits (1887),*
*Gossip on Romance* •322

*There is no longer any such*
*thing as fiction or non-fiction;*
*there's only narrative.*

**E.L. Doctorow, in** *New York Times*
*Book Review 27 January 1988* •323

*Fiction is like a spider's web,*
*attached ever so lightly perhaps,*
*but still attached to life at*
*all four corners.*

**Virginia Woolf** •324

*I abhor a mystery. I would fain, were it possible, have my tale run through from its little prologue to its customary marriage in its last chapter, with all the smoothness incidental to ordinary life. I have no ambition to surprise my reader.*

Anthony Trollope,
*The Bertrams (1859)* •325

*The novel tends to tell us everything, whereas the short story tells us only one thing, and that intensely.*

V.S. Pritchett, *attrib.* •327

*The key to a short story is tension. At the start of a short story the reader's imagination should be able to take the story on in his mind, but at the end of a novel he is entitled to expect a rounding-off.*

William Trevor, interview in
*Sunday Telegraph 21 January 1990* •326

*No human being ever spoke of scenery for above two minutes at a time, which makes me suspect we hear too much of it in literature.*

Robert Louis Stevenson,
*Memories and Portraits (1887)* •328

*To illustrate any text is also to interpret it.*

Pulitzer prize-winning writer and scholar
Alison Lurie, *Don't Tell the Grown-Ups (1990)* •329

*Illustration is a very old form, far older than the novel, balanced somewhere in between painting and literature but belonging to neither.*

Childrens author and illustrator
Shirley Hughes, *A Life Drawing (2002)* ·330

*The good ended happily, and the bad unhappily. That is what fiction means.*

Oscar Wilde, *The Importance of Being Earnest (1895)* ·331

*What the detective story is about is not murder but the restoration of order.*

P.D. James, in *Face, December 1986* ·332

*Detection is, or ought to be, an exact science, and should be treated in the same cold and unemotional manner. You have attempted to tinge it with romanticism, which produces much the same effect as if you worked a love-story or an elopement into the fifth proposition of Euclid.*

Arthur Conan Doyle, *Sherlock Holmes in The Sign of Four (1890)* ·333

*There were no innocent blondes in crime fiction.*

Ed McBain, on writing for crime magazines, in *Writers of Writing: Collected Essays from the New York Times (2001)* ·334

*How are we to account for the strange human craving for the pleasure of feeling afraid which is so much involved in our love of ghost stories?*

Virginia Woolf, in *Times Literary Supplement 31 January 1918 Across the Border* •335

*[The ghost story is] certainly the most exacting form of literary art, and perhaps the only one in which there is no immediate step between success and failure. Either it comes off or it is a flop.*

L.P. Hartley in *Cynthia Asquith (ed.) The Third Ghost Book (1955) Introduction* •338

*The tale of terror, like pornography, with which it has much in common, represents a carefree holiday from ethics.* Angela Carter, in *New Society 1975* •336

*Where there is no imagination there is no horror.*

Arthur Conan Doyle, *A Study in Scarlet (1888)* •339

*Terror… often arises from a pervasive sense of disestablishment; that things are in the unmaking.*

Stephen King, *Danse Macabre (1981)* •337

*We like to think we live in daylight, but half the world is always dark; and fantasy, like poetry, speaks the language of the night.*

Ursula Le Guin, in *World Magazine 21 November 1979* •340

*It is fortunate for tale-tellers that they are not tied down like theatrical writers to the unities of time and place.*

Sir Walter Scott, *Tales of My Landlord 1st series, (1816) Old Mortality* •341

*If some fatal process of applied science enables us in fact to reach the moon, the real journey will not at all satisfy the impulse which we now seek to gratify by writing such stories.*

C.S. Lewis, *Of Other Worlds (1966)* •342

*We need metaphors of magic and monsters in order to understand the human condition.*

Stephen Donaldson •343

*Bingo Bolger-Baggins a bad name. Let Bingo = Frodo.*

J.R.R. Tolkein does some reworking on the first draft of *Lord of the Rings*; note *c. 1938*, cited in *Humphrey Carpenter, J.R.R. Tolkein (1977)* •344

*Most modern fantasy just rearranges the furniture in Tolkein's attic.*

Terry Pratchett, in *Stan Nicholls (ed.) Wordsmiths of Wonder (1993)* •345

*Don't read science fiction books. It'll look bad if you die in bed with one on the nightstand. Always read stuff that will make you look good if you die in the middle of the night.*

P.J. ORourke, *attrib. 1979* •346

*Do you ever read what they call Science Fiction? It's a scream. It's written like this: I checked out with K19 on Adabaran III, and stepped out through the crummaliote hatch on my 22 Model Sirius Hardtop. I cocked the timejector in secondary and waded through the bright blue manda grass. My breath froze into pink pretzels. I flicked on the heat bars and the Bryllis ran swiftly on five legs using their other two to send out crylon vibrations…*

Raymond Chandler, *letter to H.N. Swanson, 14 March 1953* •347

*We live in a world where emissions from our refrigerators have caused the ozone layer to evaporate and now we'll get skin cancer if we sunbathe. If that's not a science fiction scenario, I don't know what is.*

William Gibson, *Perspectives* in *Newsweek, 5 June 1995* •348

*What is the use of a book, thought Alice, without pictures or conversations?*

Lewis Carroll, *Alice's Adventures in Wonderland (1865)* •349

*Victorian children's stories are full of children who cannot read anywhere except in a deeply embrasured window seat.*

Robertson Davies, *lecture, Yale 20 February 1990* •350

*It may be better for them to read some things, especially fairy stories, that are beyond their measure rather than short of it. Their books like their clothes should allow for growth, and their books at any rate should encourage it.*

J.R.R. Tolkein on literature for children, *Tree and Leaf (1964) On Fairy-Stories* •351

*Satire is a sort of glass, wherein beholders do generally discover everybody's face but their own; which is the chief reason for that kind of reception it meets in the world, and that so very few are offended with it.*

Jonathan Swift, *The Battle of the Books (1704), preface* •352

*Writing about travels is nearly always tedious, travelling being, like war and fornication, exciting but not interesting.*

Malcolm Muggeridge, in *Observer 5 September 1976* •353

*And what's romance? Usually, a nice little tale where you have everything As You Like It, where rain never wets your jacket and gnats never bite your nose and it's always daisy-time.*

D.H. Lawrence, *Studies in Classic American Literature (1924)* •354

*I have no problem with chick lit, I love Bridget Jones's Diary, it's just great. It's all the muck in the middle I mind… Let's have art or let's have entertainment.*

Jeanette Winterson, in *BBC News (online edition) 23 August 2001* •355

*'I am fond of history'.*
*'I wish I were too. I read it a little as a duty, but it tells me nothing that does not vex or weary me. The quarrels of popes and kings, with wars and pestilences, in every page; the men all so good for nothing, and hardly any women at all.'* Jane Austen, *Northanger Abbey (1818)* •356

It has been said that though God cannot alter the past, historians can; it is perhaps because they can be useful to Him in this respect that He tolerates their existence.

Samuel Butler, *Erewhon Revisited (1901)* ·357

Tragedy is like strong acid — it dissolves away all but the very gold of truth. D.H. Lawrence,
*letter, 1 April 1911* ·359

Whosoever, in writing a history, shall follow truth too near the heels, it may happily strike out his teeth.

Walter Ralegh, *The History of the World (1614)* ·358

Comedy is tragedy that happens to other people.

Angela Carter, *Wise Children (1991)* ·360

¶

*The bad end unhappily, the good unluckily. That is what tragedy means.*

**Tom Stoppard**, *Rosencrantz and Guildenstern are Dead (1967)* •361

*Theatre is recreation. It can be much more, but unless it's recreation, I don't see the point of it.* **Tom Stoppard, in** *Village Voice, 4 April 1995* •362

*A play, I think, ought to make sense to commonsense people. Drama is akin to other inventions of man in that it ought to help us know more, and not merely to spend our feelings.*

**Arthur Miller (with regard to his play** *The Crucible), attrib.* •363

*I've never much enjoyed going to plays… The unreality of painted people standing on a platform saying things they've said to each other for months is more than I can overlook.*

**John Updike, in** *George Plimpton (ed.) Writers at Work 4th Series (1977)* •364

*I consider it injurious for a dramatic work to be first made available to the public by a stage performance… [because it] can never be judged and understood in isolation as a piece of literature. Judgement will always include both the piece and its performance.* **Henrik Ibsen,** *letter 1872* •365

*Show me a congenital eavesdropper with the instincts of a  Peeping Tom and I will show you the makings of a dramatist.* Kenneth Tynan, *Pausing on the Stairs, 1957* •366

*A bad experience of Shakespeare is like a bad oyster — it puts you off for life.* Judi Dench •368

*At least one of my children did one of my plays at A-level. I think he got a 'B' with my help.*

Tom Stoppard on being a 'set text' author; *attrib. 1995* •367

*The play was a great success, but the audience was a total failure.*

Oscar Wilde after the first performance of *Lady Windermere's Fan,* in Peter Hay, Theatrical Anecdotes *(1987)* •369

¶

# POET'S CORNER

*Poetry's a mere drug, Sir.*

**George Farquhar,** *Love and a Bottle (1698)* ·370

*Poetry is devil's wine.*

St. Augustine, *Contra Academicos* ·373

*So poetry is something more philosophical and more worthy of serious attention than history, for while poetry is concerned with universal truths, history treats of particular facts.*

Aristotle, *Poetics* ·371

*Nature never set forth the earth in so rich tapestry as diverse poets have done... her world is brazen, the poets only deliver a golden.*

Philip Sidney, *The Defence of Poetry (1595)*·374

*So long as men can breathe, or eyes can see, So long lives this, and this gives life to thee.*

William Shakespeare, *Sonnet 18* ·375

*No verse can give pleasure for long, nor last, that is written by drinkers of water.*

Horace, *Epistles.* ·372

*For rhyme the rudder is of verses,*

*With which like ships they steer their courses.*

Samuel Butler, *Hudibras pt.1 (1663)* ·376

*The troublesome and modern bondage of rhyming.* **John Milton,** *Paradise Lost (1667) The Verse (Preface, added 1668)* •377

**Boswell:** *What is poetry?*
**Johnson:** *Why Sir, it is much easier is to say what it is not. We all know what light is; but it is not easy to tell what it is.*

**Samuel Johnson,** *Boswell, Life of Samuel Johnson (1791) 12 April 1776* •378

*Poetry, indeed, cannot be translated; and, therefore, it is poets that preserve languages; for we would not be at the trouble to learn a language, if we could have all that is written in it just as well in translation. But as the beauties of poetry cannot be preserved in any language except that in which it was originally written, we learn the language.*

**Samuel Johnson, in** *James Boswell, Life of Samuel Johnson (1791)* •380

*You will never be alone with a poet in your pocket.*

**John Adams,** *letter to John Quincy Adams, 14 May 1781* •379

*Poetry is the spontaneous overflow of powerful feelings: it takes it origin from emotion recollected in tranquility.*

**William Wordsworth,** *Lyrical Ballads (2nd ed. 1802* •381

*Iambics leap from short to long; —*
*With a leap and a bound the swift*
*  Anapaests throng.*

Samuel Taylor Coleridge,
*Metrical Feet (1806)* •382

*Whither is fled the*
*    visionary gleam?*
*Where is it now, the*
*    glory and the dream?*

William Wordsworth, *Ode. Intimations*
*of Immortality (1807)* •383

*If poetry comes not as*
*naturally as the leaves*
*to a tree it had better*
*not come at all.*

John Keats, *letter to John Taylor,*
*27 February 1818* •384

*Poetry should surprise by a fine*
*excess, and not by a singularity — it*
*should strike the reader as a wording*
*of his own highest thoughts, and*
*appear almost a remembrance.*

John Keats, *letter to John Taylor,*
*27 February 1818* •385

*Poetry is the record of the best*
*and happiest moments of the*
*happiest and best minds.*

Percy Bysshe Shelley, *A Defence*
*of Poetry (written 1821)* •386

*Prose = words in their best*
*order; — poetry = the best*
*words in the best order.*

Samuel Taylor Coleridge, *Table Talk*
*(1835), 12 July 1827* •387

*Everything you invent is true: you can be sure of that. Poetry is a subject as precise as geometry.*

Gustave Flaubert, letter to Louise Colet, 14 August 1853 •388

*We make out of the quarrel with others, rhetoric, but of the quarrel with ourselves, poetry.*

W.B. Yeats, Essays (1924) 'Anima Hominis' •391

*Prose wanders around with a lantern and laboriously schedules and verifies the details and particulars of a valley and its frame of crags and peaks, then Poetry comes, and lays bare the whole landscape with a single splendid flash.*

Mark Twain; in H.N. Smith and W.H. Gibson (eds.) Mark Twain-Howells Letters vol. 2 (1960) •389

*A poem should not mean But be.*
Archibald MacLeish, Ars Poetica (1926) •392

*Poetry is the opening and closing of a door, leaving those who look through to guess about what is seen during a moment.*

Carl Sandburg, in Atlantic Monthly March 1923 •390

*Genuine poetry can communicate before it is understood.*

T.S. Eliot, Dante (1929) •393

*As soon as war is declared it will be impossible to hold the poets back. Rhyme is still the most effective drum.*

Jean Giraudoux, *La Guerre de Troie n'aura pas lieu (1935)* •394

# Writing free verse is like playing tennis with the net down.

Robert Frost, speech on Milton Academy, Massachusetts, *1935.* •395

# Publishing a volume of poetry is like dropping a rose petal down the Grand Canyon and waiting for the echo.

Don Marquis, *Sun Dial Time (1936)* •396

*An age which is incapable of poetry is incapable of any kind of literature except the cleverness of a decadence.*

Raymond Chandler, *letter to Charles W. Morton, 5 January 1947* •397

*[Poetry] is a violence from within that protects us from a violence without.*

Wallace Stevens, *The Noble Rider And The Sounds of Words (1951)* •398

*Poetry is sissy stuff that rhymes. Weedy people sa la and fie and swoon when they see a bunch of daffodils.*

Geoffrey Willans and Ronald Searle, *Down With Skool! (1953)* •399

*Prose is when all the lines except the last go on to the end. Poetry is when some of them fall short of it.*

Jeremy Bentham, in *M. St. J. Packe, The Life of John Stuart Mill (1954)* •400

*Poetry should begin with emotion in the poet, and end with the same emotion in the reader. The poem is simply the instrument of transference.*

Philip Larkin, *BBC Third Programme, 13 April 1956* •401

*The crown of literature is poetry. It is its end and aim. It is the sublimest activity of the human mind. It is the achievement of beauty and delicacy. The writer of prose can only step aside when the poet passes.*

W. Somerset Maugham, *Saturday Review, 1957* •402

*Poetry is so emotional and very tiring.*

Edith Sitwell, *attrib. (1957)* •403

*Poetry is the revelation of a feeling that the poet believes to be interior and personal but which the reader recognizes as his own.* Salvatore Quasimodo, in *New York Times 14 May 1960* •404

*Most people ignore most poetry because most poetry ignores most people.*

Adrian Mitchell, *Poems (1964)* •405

*My favourite poem is the one that starts 'Thirty days has September' because it actually tells you something.*

Groucho Marx, in *Ned Sherrin, Cutting Edge (1984) attrib.* •406

## *Poetry is to prose as dancing is to walking.*

John Wain, talk on *BBC Radio, 1976* •407

*Novels are about other people and poems are about yourself.*

Philip Larkin, *Required Writing (1983)* •408

*I don't know why I bother really, because people don't listen to lyrics in rock'n'roll records too much.*

Lou Reed, *1989* •409

*I have emotion — no one who knows me could fail to detect it*

*But there's a serious shortage of tranquillity in which to recollect it.*

*So this is my contribution to the theoretical debate:*

*Sometimes poetry is emotion recollected in a highly emotional state.*

Wendy Cope, *An Argument with Wordsworth (1992)* •410

*Metrical poetry is ultimately allied to song, and I like the connection. Free verse is ultimately allied to conversation, and I like that connection too*

Thom Gunn, in *Paris Review 1995* •411

*Often what a poet does not say is as important as what he does.*

Miroslav Holub at a reading in Prague of Seamus Heaney's poetry, *April 1996;* in *Sunday Times 28 April 1996* •412

*There are poems about the Internet and about the shipping forecast but very few by women celebrating men.*

Germaine Greer addressing the Poetry Society. •413

*Poetry is not the most important thing in life… I'd much rather lie in a hot bath reading Agatha Christie and sucking sweets.*

Dylan Thomas, in *Joan Wyndham Love is Blue (1986) 6 July 1943* •414

¶

# All poets are mad.

Robert Burton, *The Anatomy of Melancholy
(1621-51), 'Democritus to the Reader'* •415

I am obnoxious to each
  carping tongue,
Who says my hand a needle
  better fits,
A poet's pen, all scorn, I should
  thus wrong;
Fo such despite they cast on
  female wits:
If what I do prove well, it
  won't advance,
They'll say it's stolne, or else, it
  was by chance.

Anne Bradstreet, *The Prologue (1650)* •416

Some rhyme a neebor's name
  to lash;
Some rhyme (vain thought!) for
  needfu' cash;
Some rhyme to court the
  countra clash,
An' raise a din;
For me, an aim I never fash;
  I rhyme for fun.

Robert Burns, *To J.S[mith] (1786)* •417

*The reason Milton wrote
in fetters when he wrote of
Angels and God, and at
liberty when of Devils and
Hell, is because he was a
true Poet, and of the
Devil's party without
knowing it.*

William Blake, *The Marriage
of Heaven and Hell (1790-3)* •418

*Poets are the unacknowledged legislators of the world.*

Percy Bysshe Shelley, *A Defence of Poetry (written 1821)* •419

*The poets are full of false views: they make mankind believe that happiness consists in falling in love, and living in the country —I say: live in London; like many people fall in love with nobody.*

Sydney Smith, *letter to Lady Dacre, 1837* •420

*It is beautiful; it is mournful; it is monotonous.*

Charlotte Brontë on Tennyson's *In Memoriam; letter to Mrs Gaskell, 27 August 1850* •421

*Do I contradict myself?*
*Very well then I contradict myself,*
*(I am large, I contain multitudes).*

Walt Whitman, *Song of Myself (written 1855)* •422

*Wordsworth went to the Lakes, but he never was a lake poet.. He found in stones the sermons he had already put there.*

Oscar Wilde on William Wordsworth •423

*We have been able to have fine poetry in England because the public do not read it, and consequently do not influence it. The public like to insult poets because they are individual, but once they have insulted them, they leave them alone.*

Oscar Wilde, *The Soul of Man under Socialism, 1891* •424

*All things can tempt me from this craft of verse.*

W.B. Yeats, *All Things Can Tempt Me (1909)* •425

*All a poet can do today is warn.*

First World War poet Wilfred Owen, *Preface (written 1918), Poems (1963)* •426

*Words in search of a meaning.*

Roman Jakobson, *The Newest Russian Poetry (1919; revised 1921)* •427

*Immature poets imitate; mature poets steal.*

T.S. Eliot, *The Sacred Wood (1920) Philip Massinger* •428

*Tennyson and Browning are poets, and they think; but they do not feel their thought as immediately as the odour of a rose. A thought to Donne was an experience; it modified his sensibility.*

T.S. Eliot, *The Metaphysical Poets (1921)* •429

*I am a freak user of words, not a poet. That's really the truth.*

Dylan Thomas, *letter 9 May 1934* •430

*There was a little about melancholia that he didn't know; there was little else that he did.*

W.H. Auden on Alfred, Lord Tennyson; *introduction to A Selection From the Poems of Alfred, Lord Tennyson (1947)* •431

*I am a painstaking, conscientious, involved and devious craftsman in words… I use everything to make my poems work and move in the directions I want them to: old tricks, new tricks, puns, portmanteau-words, paradox, allusion, paranomasia, paragam, catachresis, slang, assonantal rhymes, vowel rhymes, sprung rhythm...Poets have got to enjoy themselves sometimes.*

Dylan Thomas, *Poetic Manifesto (1951)* •432

*I should say that Milton's experience of propaganda is what makes his later poetry so very dramatic; that is, though he is a furious partisan, he can always imagine with all its force exactly what the reply of the opponent would be.*

William Empson, *Milton's God (1961)* •433

*The Rabbie Burns of England.*

James Knox, on John Betjeman •434

*A poet's hope: to be,*
*like some valley cheese,*
*local, but prized elsewhere.*

**W.H. Auden,** *Shorts II (1976)* •435

*When I get sent manuscripts*
*from aspiring poets, I do one*
*of two things: if there is no*
*stamp self-addressed envelope,*
*I throw it into the bin. If there is,*
*I write and tell them to fuck off.*

Philip Larkin •436

*I very much feel*
*the need to be on*
*the periphery of things.*

**Philip Larkin, in** *Observer 16 December 1979* •437

*Hughes's voice, I think, is in rebellion against a*
*certain kind of demeaned, mannerly voice... the*
*Larkin voice, the Movement voice, even the*
*Eliot voice, the Auden voice – the manners of*
*that speech, the original voices behind that*
*poetic voice, are those of literate middle-class*
*culture, and I think Hughes's great cry and call*
*and bawl is that English language and English*
*poetry is longer and deeper than that.*

**Seamus Heaney, in** *John Haffendn (ed.)*
*Viewpoints (1981)* •438

*I would have a poet able-bodied,*
*fond of talking, a reader of the*
*newspapers, capable of pity and*
*laughter, informed in economics,*
*appreciative of women, involved*
*in personal relationships, actively*
*interested in politics, susceptible*
*to physcial impressions.*

**Louis MacNeice,** *Modern Poetry (1938).*
Not asking much... •439

*She wrote her early poems very slowly, thesaurus open on her knee… chewing her lips, putting a thick dark ring of ink around each word that stirred her on the page of the thesaurus.*

Ted Hughes on his wife Sylvia Plath, in *Seamus Heaney, Finders Keepers (2002)* •440

*The only poets with full-time salaries earn them at greeting-card companies.*

Bill Thomas, in *Los Angeles Times 13 January 1991* •441

*In no other job have I ever had to deal with such utterly abnormal people. Yes, it is true, poetry does something to them.*

Muriel Spark, on working for the Poetry Society; *Curriculum Vitae (1992)* •442

*The poetry world is very small and full of green-eyed snapping fish.*

Andrew Motion •443

*Poets or artists are sometimes married very happily to their muse; and sometimes they have a very difficult life with her.*

W.H. Auden, in conversation with Isaiah Berlin, *Daily Telegraph 3 August 1996* •444

*I used think all poets*
*were Byronic — mad,*
*bad and dangerous*
*to know. And then*
*I met a few. They're*
*mostly wicked as*
*ginless tonic and wild*
*as pension plans.*

Wendy Cope ·445

¶

# *THE CRITICAL MOMENTS*

*People ask you for criticism, but they only want praise.*

**W. Somerset Maugham,**
*Of Human Bondage (1915)* ·446

*Whom the Gods wish to destroy they first call promising.*

Cyril Connolly, *Enemies of Promise, 1938* •447

*Criticism is a study by which men grow important and formidable at very small expense.*

Samuel Johnson, in *The Idler 9 June 1759*•448

*People who like this sort of thing will find this the sort of thing they like.*

Abraham Lincoln's judgement of a book, in *G.W.E. Russell, Collections and Recollections (1898)* •449

*If they [writers] believe the critics when they say they are great then they must believe them when they say they are rotten and they lose confidence.*

Ernest Hemingway, *Green Hills of Africa (1935)* •450

*I am strongly of opinion that an author had far better not read any reviews of his books: the unfavourable ones are almost certain to make him cross, and the favourable ones conceited; and neither of these results is desirable.*

Lewis Carroll, *Sylvie and Bruno Concluded (1893)* •451

The
Nature
of
Criticism

*They [writers] fret over savage reviews because rejection of their work… means rejection of themselves and of their working lives… However, it is clear that no review, no matter how bad or how unfair, can seriously injure the sales of a book if the public desires to read it.*

Irving Wallace, *The Writing of One Novel (1968)* •452

*It is the nature of the artist to mind excessively what is said about him. Literature is strewn with the wreckage of men who have minded beyond reason the opinions of others.* Virginia Woolf,
*A Room of One's Own, 1929* •455

*There's no such thing as bad publicity except your own obituary.*

Brendan Behan, Irish playwright, in
*Dominic Behan, My Brother Brendan (1965)* •453

*If it is abuse, — why one is always sure to hear of it from one damned good natured friend or another!*

Richard Brinsley Sheridan,
*The Critic (1779)* •454

*No critical display is more offensive than that which praises one author by damning another, as though critical judgement were a seesaw on which one reputation cannot rise unless another is lowered.*

Carolyn G. Heilbrun, *Hamlet's Mother and Other Women (1990) 'Virginia Woolf and James Joyce'* •456

*With all those prizes the most interesting thing is getting on the shortlist, because that tells you who people see as your peers.*

David Malouf, in *Daily Telegraph 7 September 1996* •457

*I will try to account for the degree of my aesthetic emotion. That, I conceive, is the function of the critic.*

Clive Bell, *Art (1914)* •458

*That one book is better than another is nothing more than a matter of taste. I find it difficult to accept that it's something that can be decided by a panel of judges.*

Graham Swift, in *Observer 24 June 1990 'Sayings of the Week'* •459

*This is an important book, the critic assumes, because it deals with war. This is an insignificant book because it deals with the feelings of women in a drawing-room.*

Virginia Woolf, *A Room of One's Own (1929)* •460

*The whole idea of an award just for women fills me with horror.*

Anita Brookner voices her opposition to the Orange Prize for women's fiction, in *Sunday Times 21April 1996* •461

*Some of the editors wrote rejection slips that were more creative than anything I had written. On my tenth submission to Redbook… 'Mrs Clark, your stories are light, slight, and trite.' My first novella was returned with the succinct note: 'We found the heroine as boring as her husband had.'*

Mary Higgins Clark, in *The Writing Life: Collection from Washington Post Book World (2003)* •462

*You may abuse a tragedy, though you cannot write one. You may scold a carpenter who has made you a bad table, though you cannot make a table. It is not  your trade to make tables.*

Samuel Johnson, in *James Boswell, Life of Samuel Johnson (1791) 25 June 1763* •463

*Every genius needs praise.*

Gertrude Stein, in *Edmund White,
The Burning Library (1994)*•464

¶

*A critic is a man who knows the way but can't drive the car.*

Kenneth Tynan, in *New York Times Magazine*
*9 January 1966* •465

Criticism is a life without risk.

John Lahr, *Light·Fantastic (1996)* •467

There is, perhaps, no more dangerous
man in the world than the man with
the sensibilities of an artist but without
creative talent. With luck such men
make wonderful theatrical impresarios
and interior decorators, or else they
become mass murderers or critics.

Barry Humphries, *More Please (1992)* •466

*A man is a critic when he cannot be an artist, in the same way that a man becomes an informer when he cannot be a soldier.*

Gustave Flaubert, *letter to Louise Colet*
*(1846)* •468

*A good writer is not per se a good book critic. No more than a good drunk is automatically a good bartender.* Jim Bishop, in

New York Journal-American, November 1957 •469

*A true critic ought to dwell rather upon excellencies than imperfections, to discover the concealed beauties of a writer, and communicate to the world such things as are worth their observation.*

Joseph Addison, *The Spectator* 2 February 1712 •470

# *A sneer of critics.*

Peter Nichols coins a collective noun, Diary 6 February 1974 •471

*Western man, especially the Western critic, still finds it very hard to go into print and say: 'I recommend you go to see this because it gave me an erection'.* Kenneth Tynan,

Playboy, 1977 •472

*Though it often apes scientific language, critical theory would not be recognized as theory by any scientist, since it does not open itself up to experimental verification. Composed purely of assertions, not testable hypotheses, it can have no bearing on reality, and no explanatory value.*

John Carey, in *Sunday Times* 7 August 1994 •473

*I never read a book before reviewing it; it prejudices a man so.*

Sydney Smith, in *H. Pearson, The Smith of Smiths (1934)* •474

*Asking a playwright how he felt about critics was like asking a lamppost how it felt about dogs.*

Christopher Hampton, in *The Times 4 April 1995* •475

¶

*He was not of an age, but for all time!*

Ben Jonson, *To the Memory of My Beloved, the Author, Mr William Shakespeare (1623)* •476

*In his plays you often find remarks doing a kitchen-hand's work in some remote corner of a sentence which would deserve pride of place in a disquisition by any other writer.*

Georg Christoph Lichtenberg, *notebooks 1765-99* •477

*Was there ever such stuff as great part of Shakespeare? Only one must not say so! But what think you? — what? — Is there not sad stuff? what — what?* George III, to Fanny Burney, *Diary, 19 December 1785* •478

*It is said that Shakespeare depicted the Romans superbly. I don't see this. They are sheer, inveterate Englishmen, but they are truly human, fundamentally human, and so the Roman toga suits them well enough.*

Johann Wolfgang von Goethe, *Shakespeare without End (1815)* •479

*He was not a man, he was a continent; he contained whole crowds of men, entire landscapes.*

Gustave Flaubert on Shakespeare, *letter, 19 September 1852* •480

*Fantastic! And it was all written with a feather!*

American film producer Sam Goldwyn on the works of Shakespeare; *attrib.,* in *John Gross, After Shakespeare (2002)* •481

*The remarkable thing about Shakespeare is that he really is very good, in spite of all the people who say he is very good.*

Robert Graves, *1964* •482

*There is a sense in which every writer in English owes a debt to Shakespeare. He is our theatrical DNA.*

Richard Eyre, *Changing Stages, BBC2 TV, 5 November 2000* •483

*To escape from the grotesque tragedy which was his body, Pope perfected a series of immaculate masks and voices.*

John Carey, in *Sunday Times 1985* •484

*This man… who has the most extensive knowledge, the clearest understanding, and the greatest abilities of any living author, — has a face the most ugly, a person the most awkward, and manners the most singular, that ever were, or ever can be seen. But all that is unfortunate in his exterior, is so greatly compensated for in his interior, that I can only, like Desdemona to Othello, 'see his visage in his mind'.* Fanny Burney, of Samuel Johnson, *letter to her sister Susan, August 1778* •485

*I am in the path of Blake, but so far behind him that only the wings of his heels are in sight.*

Dylan Thomas, *letter to Pamela Hansford Johnson, undated, probably September 1933* •486

*He talked on for ever; and you wished him to talk on for ever.*

William Hazlitt on Coleridge, *Lectures on the English Poets (1818)* •487

*The owner of a mind which keeps open house, and entertains all comers.*

William Hazlitt on Coleridge, *The Spirit of the Age (1825)* •488

*Walter Scott has no business to write novels, especially good ones — It is not fair. — He has fame and profit enough as a poet, and should not be taking the bread out of other people's mouths. — I do not like him, and do not mean to like Waverley if I can help it — but fear I must.*

Jane Austen, *letter to Anna Austen, 28 September 1814* •489

*The Big Bow-Wow strain I can do myself like any now going; but the exquisite touch, which renders ordinary commonplace things and characters interesting, from the truth of the description and the sentiment, is denied to me.*

Sir Walter Scott compares himself to Jane Austen, in W.E.K. Anderson (ed.), *Journals of Sir Walter Scott (1972) 14 March 1826* •490

*Shelley is truth itself — and honour itself — notwithstanding his out-of-the-way notions about religion.*

Lord Byron on Percy Bysshe Shelley, *letter to Douglas Kinnaird, 2 June 1821* •491

*Hair in disorder, eyes lost in a dream, a genius who, in his little room, is able to reconstruct bit by bit the entire structure of his society and to expose life in all its tumultuousness for his contemporaries and for all generations to come.*

Auguste Rodin on Balzac, in *L'Art et les artistes, February 1900* •492

*Balzac observed all the things that Marx did not.*

Régis Debray, *Teachers, Writers, Celebrities (1981) 'Balzac, or Zoology Today'* •493

*He had a large loving mind and the strongest sympathy with the poorest classes. He felt sure a better feeling, and much greater union of classes, would take place in time. And I pray earnestly it may.*

Queen Victoria, *Diary 11 June 1870; on Charles Dickens.* •494

*He describes London like a special correspondent for posterity.* Walter Bagehot, of Charles Dickens, in *National Review 7 October 1858,* 'Charles Dickens' •495

*My own experience in reading Dickens… is to be bounced between violent admiration and violent distaste almost every couple of paragraphs, and this is too uncomfortable a condition to be much allievated by an inward recital of one's not to be fastidious, to gulp the stuff down in gobbets like a man.*

Kingsley Amis, *What Became of Jane Austen? (1970)* •496

*It does not matter that Dickens' world is not lifelike; it is alive.*

Lord David Cecil, *Early Victorian Novelists (1978)* •497

*We were put to Dickens as children but it never quite took. That unremitting humanity soon had me cheesed off.* Alan Bennett, *The Old Country (1978)* •498

*He remains in many ways the foremost prophet of our time...There is no one today with Tolstoy's deep insight and moral force.*

Albert Einstein, interview in *Survey Graphic August 1934* •499

*He was as fond of me as he could be of anyone over the age of ten.*

Ellen Terry on Lewis Carroll, in *Derek Hudson, Lewis Carroll* •500

*Thackeray is like the edited and illustrated edition of a great dinner.*

Walter Bagehot, in *Spectator 9 August 1862* •501

*His first, his inestimable merit was a complete appreciation of the usual.*

Henry Jameson on Anthony Trollope, *Partial Portraits (1888)* •502

*All modern American literature comes from one book by Mark Twain called Huckleberry Finn.*

Ernest Hemingway, *Green Hills of Africa (1935)* •503

*Children swarmed to him like settlers. He became a land.*

W.H. Auden on English artist and writer of humourous verse Edward Lear; *Edward Lear (1939)* •504

*From the beginning Wilde performed his life and continued to do so even after fate had taken the plot out of his hands.* W.H. Auden, in

*New Yorker 9 March 1963* •505

*Chekhov made a mistake in thinking that if he had had more time he would have written more fully, described the rain, and the midwife and the doctor having tea. The truth is one can only get so much into a story; there is always a sacrifice. One has to leave out what one knows and longs to use.*

Katherine Mansfield on fellow short story-writer Anton Chekhov, *Diary, 1922* •506

*I do not think Shaw will be a great literary figure in 2000AD. He is an amazingly brilliant contemporary; but he is not in the Hardy class.*

Harold Nicolson, *Diary 11 December 1950* •507

*He is a most remarkable man — and I am the other one. Between us we cover all knowledge; he knows all that can be known and I know the rest.*

Mark Twain, about Rudyard Kipling, *Autobiography (1924)* •508

*His virtuosity with language is not unlike that of one of his drill sergeants with an awkward squad… The vulgarest words learn to wash behind their ears and to execute complicated movements at the word of command, but they can hardly be said to learn to think for themselves.*

W.H. Auden, re Kipling, in *New Republic* 24 October 1943 •509

*One could always baffle Conrad by saying 'humour'. It was one of our damned English tricks he had never learned to tackle.*

H.G. Wells on Joseph Conrad •510

*Whatever Wells writes is not only alive, but kicking.*

Henry James on English novelist H.G. Wells, in *G.K. Chesterton, Autobiography (1936)* •511

*He's the Shakespeare of science fiction.*

Brian Aldiss on H.G. Wells, on *Bookmark (BBC2) 24 August 1996* •512

*Chesterton had a body like a slag heap, but a mind like the dawn sky. He saw the world new, as if he'd just landed from another planet.*

John Carey, in *Sunday Times 1978* •513

An essentially private man, who wished his total indifference to public notice to be universally recognized. Tom Stoppard on James Joyce •514

His writing is not about something. It is the thing itself.

Samuel Beckett, of James Joyce, *Our Exagmination Round His Factification for Incamination of Work in Progress (1929)* •515

Few if any of the great novelists are people one would like to know as friends. Hemingway the bully; Proust the snob; Waugh the snobbish bully; Fitzgerald the drunk; Dickens the exhibitionist — they are all great novelists because they like to exploit and manipulate people, to mock and devastate people, to torment and trample on people — and we are talking, remember, of people they have themselves created.

Kenneth Tynan, *Diary, 7 January 1972* •516

I was jealous of her writing — the only writing I have ever been jealous of.

Virginia Woolf, of Katherine Mansfield, shortly after the New Zealand writer's death; *letter, 16 January 1923* •517

*Kafka could never have written as he did had he lived in a house. His writing is that of someone whose whole life was spent in apartments, with lifts, stairwells, muffled voices behind closed doors, and sounds through walls. Put him in a nice detached villa and he'd never have written a word.*

Alan Bennett on Czech novelist and short story writer Franz Kafka, *Writing Home (1994)* •518

*Wherever one cut him, with a little question, he poured, spurted fountains of ideas.*

Virginia Woolf on W.B. Yeats, *Diary, 8 November 1930* •519

*He wrote like God. He could put words together with such certainty that they seem to have been graven on tablets of stone from the beginning of time.*

John Carey on W.B. Yeats; *Pure Pleasure (2000)* •520

*Your novels beat me — black and blue… Of course I admire your creative work immensely — but only in a bemused and miserable manner.* Max Beerbohm, in a *letter to Virginia Woolf, 30 December 1927* •521

*I believe in the established canon of English and American literature and in the validity of the concept of privileged texts. I think it is more important to read Spenser, Shakespeare, or Milton than to read Borges in translation, or even, to say the truth, to read Virginia Woolf.*

J. Hillis Miller, in *Sandra M. Gilbert, What Do Feminist Critics Want? (1980)* •522

You praise the firm restraint
  with which they write —
I'm with you there, of course:
They use the snaffle and the
  curb all right,
But where's the bloody horse?

Roy Campbell, 'On Some South African
Novelists' (1930) •523

An elderly fallen angel
travelling incognito.

Peter Quennell on French novelist
and critic André Gide, *The Sign of
the Fish* (1960) •524

As a man, he combines
the manner of Friar
Tuck with mind of
St. Augustine.

Kenneth Tynan on C.S. Lewis,
*Persona Grata* (1953) •525

Agatha Christie has given
more pleasure in bed than
any other woman.

Nancy Banks-Smith •526

He is a subtle poet, but
not a sophisticated one.

Philip Larkin on John Betjeman, *Further
Requirements* (2001) •527

Betjeman's cachet is by now that
of a cherished public monument.
It would be only mildly surprising
to hear that he had been acquired
by the National Trust.

John Carey, in *Sunday Times*
*9 January 1983* •528

He is both glum and funny,
a mixture the English
always find endearing.

John Carey on Alan Bennett, in
*Sunday Times 9 October 1994* •529

Coleridge was a drug addict.
Poe was an alcoholic.
Marlowe was stabbed by
a man whom he was
treacherously trying to
stab. Pope took money
to keep a woman's name
out of a satire then wrote
a piece so that she could
be recognized anyhow.
Chatterton killed himself.
Byron was accused of incest.
Do you still want to become
a writer — and if so, why?

Bennett Cerf, *Shake Well*
*Before Using* (1948) •530

¶

# THE ENVENOMED PEN

*Mr Gladstone read Homer for fun,*
*which I thought served him right.*

**Winston Churchill,** *My Early Life (1930)* ·531

*A Methodist parson in Bedlam.*

Horace Walpole on Dante ·532

*A strange horrible business, but I suppose good enough for Shakespeare's day.*

Queen Victoria giving her opinion of *King Lear* ·533

*Prince Hamlet thought Uncle a traitor for having it off with his mother; revenge Dad or not? That's the gist of the plot, and he did — nine soliloquies later.*

Stanley J., Sharpless, *New Statesman* ·534

*All through the five acts… he played the King as though under momentary apprehension that someone else was about to play the Ace.*

Eugene Field, reviewing Creston Clarke's *King Lear, Denver Tribune, 1880* ·535

*Crude, immoral, vulgar and senseless.*

Leo Tolstoy, on William Shakespeare ·536

*I have tried lately to read Shakespeare, and found it so intolerably dull that it nauseated me.*

Charles Darwin on William Shakespeare ·537

*Shakespeare never had six lines together without a fault. Perhaps you may find seven, but this does not refute my general assertion.*

Samuel Johnson on William Shakespeare ·538

# This enormous dunghill.

Voltaire, on William Shakespeare •539

With the single exception of Homer, there is no eminent writer, not even Sir Walter Scott, whom I can despise so entirely as I despise Shakespeare when I measure my mind against his.

George Bernard Shaw in *Saturday Review 2 6 September 1896* •540

The basis of all Bernard Shaw's attacks on Shakespeare is really the charge — quite true, of course — that Shakespeare wasn't an enlightened member of the Fabian society.

George Orwell, in *Listener 19 March 1942* •541

To the King's theatre, where we saw 'A Midsummer Night's Dream' which I had never seen before nor shall ever again for it is the most insipid, ridiculous play that I ever saw in my life.

Entry in Samuel Pepys' *Diary* •542

The comedies of Ben Jonson are clearly no laughing matter if we compare them with Shakespeare.

Nevill Coghill, *Collected Papers of Nevill Coghill (1988) The Basis of Shakespearean Comedy* •543

A play of Webster's is full of the feverish and ghastly turmoil of a nest of maggots.

Rupert Brooke, *John Webster and Elizabethan Drama (1916)* •544

*Paradise Lost is one of those books which the readers admires, lays down and forgets to take up again. Its perusal is a duty rather than a pleasure.*

Samuel Johnson, *Lives of the English Poets (1779-81) Milton* •545

*A vain, silly, transparent coxcomb without either solid talents or a solid nature.* J.G. Lockhart on Samuel Pepys •546

*A monster gibbering shrieks, and gnashing imprecations against mankind — tearing down all shreds of modesty, past all sense of manliness and shame; filthy in word, filthy in thought, furious, raging, obscene.*

William Makepeace Thackeray on Jonathan Swift, author of *Gulliver's Travels* •547

*Why, Sir, if you were to read Richardson for the story, your impatience would be so much fretted that you would hang yourself.*

Samuel Johnson on (interminable) English novelist Samuel Richardson, in *James Boswell, Life of Samuel Johnson (1791) '6 April 1772'* •548

*He was dull in a new way that made people think him great.*

Samuel Johnson, on poet Thomas Gray; in Boswell's *Life of Samuel Johnson (1791) ''28 March 1775'* •549

*If you imagine a Scotch commercial traveller in a Scotch commercial hotel on the bar and calling the barmaid Dearie, then you will know the keynote of Burns' verse.* A.E. Housman ·550

*An Archangel a little damaged.*

Charles Lamb on Samuel Taylor Coleridge, letter to Wordsworth, 26 April 1816 ·552

*Mad, bad, and dangerous to know.*

Lady Charles Lamb's assessment, in her diary, of Lord Byron after their first meeting at a ball in March 1812 ·553

*Mr Wordsworth, a stupid man, with a decided gift for portraying nature in vignettes, never ruined anyone's morals, unless perhaps, he has driven some susceptible persons to crime in a very fury of boredom.* Ezra Pound, on William Wordsworth ·551

*Always looking at himself in mirrors to make sure he was sufficiently outrageous.*

Enoch Powell on Lord Byron, Sunday Times 8 May 1988 ·554

*I never heard a single expression of fondness for him fall from the lips of any of those who knew him well.*

Lord Macaulay on Lord Byron, letter 7 June 1831 •555

*Sir Walter Scott, when all is said and done, is an inspired butler.*

William Hazlitt •558

*The world is rid of Lord Byron, but the deadly slime of his touch still remains.*

John Constable, artist, on news of Bryon's death •556

*A fat little flabby person with the face of a baker, the clothes of a cobbler, the size of a barrelmaker, the manners of a stocking salesman, and the dress of an innkeeper.* Victor de Balabin on Honore de Balzac •559

*[Frankenstein is] a book about what happens when a man tries to have a baby without a woman.*

Anne K. Mellor, in *Sunday Correspondent* 8 April 1990 •557

*He has occassional flashes of silence, that make his conversation perfectly delightful.*

Sydney Smith of Lord Macaulay, English politician and historian; in *Lady Holland, Memoir, vol.1 (1855)* •560

It is a long yet vigorous, like the penis of a jackass.

Sydney Smith on an article in the
*Edinburgh Review by Harry Brougham* ·561

Carlyle is a poet to whom nature has denied the faculty of verse.

Alfred, Lord Tennyson, *letter to
W.E. Gladstone, c.1870* ·562

All the faults of Jane Eyre are magnified a thousand, and the only consolation which we have in reflecting upon it is that it will never be generally read.

James Lorimer on *Wuthering Heights* by
Emily Brontë, in the *North British Review* ·563

Longfellow is to poetry what the barrel-organ is to music. Van Wyck Brooks on Henry
Wadsworth Longfellow ·564

I can never remember if Moby Dick is the man or the whale.

James Thurber ·565

*He was unperfect, unfinished, inartistic; he was worse than provincial — he was parochial.*

Henry James on Henry David Thoreau •566

*A dirty man with opium-glazed eyes and rat-taily hair.*

Lady Frederick Cavendish on Tennyson •569

*One must have a heart of stone to read the death of little Nell without laughing.*

Oscar Wilde on Charles Dickens'
*Old Curiosity Shop* •567

*Walt Whitman is as unacquainted with art as a hog with mathematics.*

London Critic on Walt Whitman •570

*A louse in the locks of literature.*

Presumably critic John Churton Collins had done something to upset Alfred, Lord Tennyson; in *Evan Charteris, 'Life and Letters of Sir Edmund Gosse' (1931)* •568

*The awful Whitman. This post-mortem poet. This poet with the private soul leaking out of him all the time. All his privacy leaking out in a sort pf dribble, oozing into the universe.*

D. H. Lawrence, on Walt Whitman •571

# Nothing but a pack of lies.

Damon Runyon doesn't quite 'get' *Alice in Wonderland* •572

*She is magnificently ugly — deliciously hideous. She has a low forehead, a dull grey eye, a vast pendulous nose… Now in this vast ugliness resides a most powerful beauty which, in a very few minutes steals forth and charms the mind, so that you end as I ended, in falling in love with her. Yes behold me literally in love with this great horse-faced blue-stocking.*

Henry James finds a peculiar fascination in George Eliot; *letter 10 May 1869* •573

*Arnold is a dandy Isaiah, a poet without passion, whose verse, written in surplice, is for freshmen and for gentle maidens who will be wooed to the arms of these future rectors.*

George Meredith on the poet and essayist Matthew Arnold, in *Fortnightly Review July 1909* •574

# Of course we all know that Morris was a wonderful all-round man, but the act of walking round him has always tired me.

Max Beerbohm on William Morris •575

*Henry James writes fiction as if it was a painful duty.*

Oscar Wilde ·576

*Poor Henry James! He's spending eternity walking round and round a stately park and the fence is just too high for him to peep over and he's just too far away to hear what the countess is saying.*

W. Somerset Maugham ·577

*I am reading Henry James… and feel myself as one entombed in a block of smooth amber.* Virginia Woolf on Henry James ·578

*A hack writer who would not have been considered fourth rate in Europe, who tried out a few of the old proven 'sure-fire' literary skeletons with sufficient local colour to intrigue the superficial and the lazy.*

William Faulkner on Mark Twain ·579

*No I've never cared for his work. Too scented.*

Rudyard Kipling on the works of Oscar Wilde; in *Harry Ricketts, The Unforgiving Minute (1999)* ·580

*Kipling is a Jingo imperialist, he is morally insensitive and aesthically disgusting.*

George Orwell ·581

He hasn't an enemy in the world, and none of his friends like him.

Oscar Wilde on George Bernard Shaw ·582

Conrad spent a day finding the mot juste; then killed it.

Ford Madox Ford, in *Robert Lowell, Notebook 1967-68 (1969)* ·584

What is Conrad but the wreck of Stevenson floating about in the slipsop of Henry James.

George Moore, on Joseph Conrad ·583

As a contribution to natural history the work is negligible.

E.V. Lucas in a review of Kenneth Grahame's *Wind in the Willows;* in *Times Literary Supplement 22 October 1908* ·585

He is limp and damp and milder than the breath of a cow.

Virginia Woolf on E.M. Forster ·586

*Spit on her when you see her, she's a liar out and out. As for him, I reserve my language... vermin, the pair of 'em.*

D.H. Lawrence on Katherine Mansfield and J. Middleton Murray •587

*He writes the worst English that I have ever encountered. It reminds me of a string of wet sponges; it reminds me of tattered washing on the line; it reminds me of stale bean soup, of college yells, or dogs barking idiotically through endless nights.*

H.L. Mencken, on US President Warren G, Harding, *Baltimore Evening Sun, 1921* •588

## The work of a queasy undergraduate scratching his pimples.

Virginia Woolf on *Ulysses* by James Joyce •589

*So you've been reviewing Sitwell's last piece of Virgin dung, have you? Isn't she a poisonous thing of a woman, lying, concealing, flipping, plagiarising, misquoting, and being as clever a crooked literary publicist as ever.*

Dylan Thomas on Edith Sitwell •590

*Mr Lawrence looked like a plaster gnome on a stone toadstool in some suburban garden... he looked as if he had just returned from spending an uncomfortable night in a very dark cave.*

Dame Edith Sitwell, on D.H. Lawrence •591

*He's impossible. He's pathetic and preposterous. He writes like a sick man.*

Gertrude Stein, on D.H. Lawrence •592

*This fictional account of the day-by-day life of an English gamekeeper is still of considerable interest to outdoor-minded readers, as it contains many passages on pheasant raising, the apprehending of poachers, ways to control vermin, and other chores and duties of the professional gamekeeper. Unfortunately one is obliged to wade through many pages of extraneous material in order to discover and savour these sidelights on the management of a Midlands shooting estate, and in this reviewer's opinion this book cannot take the place of J.R. Miller's 'Practical Gamekeeping'.*

An anonymous reviewer rather misses the point of D.H. Lawrence's *Lady Chatterley's Lover; attributed to* Field and Stream, c.1928 •593

*You could always tell by his conversation which volume of the Encyclopedia Britannica he'd been reading. One day it would be the Alps, Andes and Apennines, and the next it would be the Himalayas and the Hippocratic Oath.*

Bertrant Russell on Aldous Huxley; letter to R.W. Clark, July 1965 •594

*I enjoyed talking to her, but thought nothing of her writing. I considered her a beautiful little knitter.*

Dame Edith Sitwell on Virginia Woolf •595

*Personally, I would rather have written Winnie-the-Pooh than the collected works of Brecht.*

Tom Stoppard, *attrib. 1972* •596

## Actually I loathed the Viennese Quack

Vladimir Nabokov, on Sigmund Freud ·597

*To see Stephen Spender fumbling with our rich and delicate language is to experience all the horror of seeing a Servres vase in the hands of a chimpanzee.*

Evelyn Waugh ·598

*He gave pleasure a bad name.*

E.M. Forster on English writer and critic
Cyril Connolly, in *Noël Annan, Our Age (1990)* ·599

*He has never been known to use a word that might send a man to a dictionary.*

William Faulkner, on Ernest Hemingway ·600

*He could not blow his nose without moralising on the state of the handkerchief industry.*

Cyril Connolly on George Orwell, in
*Sunday Times 29 September 1968* ·601

## Oh really. What exactly is she reading?

## My face looks like a wedding cake that has been left out in the rain.

W.H. Auden on himself •604

## The punctuation is pitiable but it never becomes unintelligible so I just shouldn't try. It is clearly not your subject — like theology.

Evelyn Waugh in a *letter to Nancy Mitford,* re her *Love in a Cold Climate, 24 October 1948* •603

It has taken 33 years for Jean-Paul Sartre's 'The Devil and the Good Lord' to reach London, but our luck was bound to run out sooner or later.

Kenneth Hurren, in *The Mail on Sunday* •605

## A play in which nothing happens, twice.

Vivian Mercier, reviewing Beckett's *Waiting for Godot* in *Irish Times, 1954* •606

# Jack Kerouac? That's not writing that's typing.

Truman Capote ·607

The trouble with Ian Fleming is that he gets off with women because he can't get on with them.

English novelist Rosamund Lehmann borrows a line from Elizabeth Bowen in her assessment of the *James Bond* author; in *J. Pearson, The Life of Ian Fleming (1966)* ·608

When it comes down to it, 'Lucky Jim' is 'Just William', bigger and bespectacled, literate and funny, but scarcely grown-up.

Simon Gray on Kingsley Amis' *Lucky Jim*, in *The Times* *3 February 1966* ·609

To a Hollywood writer who had criticised the work of Alan Bennett: 'Listen, dear, you couldn't write fuck on a dusty venetian blind.

English actress Coral Browne; *attrib., in Sunday Times Magazine 1984* ·610

*He can't write fiction and he can't write non-fiction, so he's invented a bogus category in between.*

Ian Hislop, on Jeffrey Archer's new 'novelography'; in *Observer* 14 April 1996 'Sayings of the Week' •611

*He was not a serious politician. But his footwork should command respect. He is proof of the proposition that in each of us lurks one bad novel.*

Julian Critchley on Jeffrey Archer •612

*Last time I went to Portugal I got through six Jeffrey Archer novels. I must remember to take enough toilet paper next time.*

Bob Monkhouse •613

*So boring you
fall asleep halfway
through her name.*

Alan Bennett on Arianna Stassinopoulos
in the *Observer* •614

¶

Spleen

*Any kiddie in school
  can love like a fool,*

*But hating, my boy,
  is an art.*

Ogden Nash, *Plea for Less
Malice Toward None (1933)* •615

*There's no possibility of being
witty without a little ill-nature;
the malice of a good thing is
the barb that makes it stick.*

Richard Brinsley Sheridan,
*The School for Scandal (1777)* •617

*People wish their enemies
dead — but I do not; I say
give them the gout, give
them the stone!*

Lady Mary Wortley Montagu, in
*W.S. Lewis et al, eds., Horace Walpole's
Correspondence vol.35 (1973)* •616

*I like to write when I feel spiteful;
it's like having a good sneeze.*

D.H. Lawrence, *letter to Lady Cynthia
Asquith, c.25 November 1913* •618

*Nowadays, a parlour maid as ignorant as Queen Victoria was when she came to the throne would be classed as mentally defective.*

George Bernard Shaw on Queen Victoria •619

*I can't help detesting my relations. I suppose it comes from the fact that none of us can stand other people having the same faults as ourselves.*

Oscar Wilde, *The Picture of Dorian Gray, 1891* •620

*Writers are always envious, mean-minded, filled with rage and envy at others' good fortune. There is nothing like the failure of a close friend to cheer us up.* Peter Carey, in *Observer 18 August 2002* •621

*Your manuscript is both good and original; but the part that is good is not original, and the part that is original is not good.*

Samuel Johnson •622

*The covers of this book are too far apart.*

Ambrose Bierce, *Review* •623

*This is not a novel to be tossed aside lightly. It should be thrown with great force.*

Dorothy Parker, in *R.E. Drennan, Wit's End* •624

*All women, as authors, are feeble and tiresome. I wish they were forbidden to write, on pain of having their faces deeply scarified with an oyster shell.* Nathaniel Hawthorne, *letter to his publisher, 1852* •625

*Mrs Portman is not much admired in Dorsetshire; the good-natured world as usual extolled her beauty so highly that all the neighbourhood have had the pleasure of being disappointed.*

Jane Austen, *Letter to her sister, Cassandra* •626

*I spent Friday evening with the Mapletons, and was obliged to submit to being pleased in spite of my inclination.*

Jane Austen, *Letter to her sister, Cassandra* •627

*Mrs Hall of Sherbourne was brought to bed yesterday of a dead child, some weeks before she expected, owing to a fright. I suppose she happened to look unawares at her husband.*

Jane Austen, *letter* •628

*Poor woman! how can she (Mrs Tilson) honestly be breeding again?*

Jane Austen, *Letter to her sister, Cassandra* •629

*Only think of Mrs Holder's being dead! Poor woman, she has done the only thing in the world she could possibly do to make one cease to abuse her.*

Jane Austen, *Letter to her sister, Cassandra* •630

*If Mrs Freeman is anywhere above ground give my best compliments to her.*

Jane Austen, *Letter to her sister, Cassandra* •631

*Nearly all bookish people are snobs, and especially the more englightened among them. They are apt to assume that if a writer has immense circulation, if he is enjoyed by plain persons, and if he can fill several theatres at once, he cannot possibly be worth reading and merits only indifference and disdain.*

Arnold Bennett, in *Evening Standard 19 July 1928* •632

*Sapper, Buchan, Dornford Yates, practitioners in that school of Snobbery with Violence that runs like a thread of good-class tweed through twentieth-century literature.*

Alan Bennett, *Forty Years On (1969)* •633

## Most writers have the egotism of actors with none of the good looks or charm.

Raymond Chandler, *letter to Leonore Offord, December 1948* •634

*I hate vulgar realism in literature. The man who would call a spade a spade should be compelled to use one. It is the only thing he is fit for.*

Oscar Wilde, *The Picture of Dorian Gray, 1891* •635

## The media. It sounds like a convention of spiritualists.

Tom Stoppard, *Night and Day (1978)* •636

*You cannot hope to bribe or twist, thank God! the British journalist. But, seeing what the man will do unbribed, there's no occasion to.*

Humbert Wolfe, *Over the Fire (1930)* •637

*Journalists say a thing that they know isn't true, in the hope that if they keep on saying it long enough it will be true.*

Arnold Bennett, *The Title (1918)* •638

*The only qualities essential for real success in journalism are ratlike cunning, a plausible manner, and a little literary ability… [and]… the capacity to steal other people's ideas and phrases — that one about ratlike cunning was invented by my colleage Murray Sayre — is also invaluable.*

English journalist Nicholas Tomalin, in *Poison Penmanship: The Gentle Art of Muckraking (1979)* •639

*The newspapers! Sir, they are the most villainous — licentious — abominable — infernal — Not that I ever read them — No — I make it a rule never to look into a newspaper.*

Richard Brinsley Sheridan, *The Critic (1779)* •640

*What makes me qualified to be a reporter? Well, I'm willing to violate anyone's privacy for my personal gain and then claim with a straight face that the public has a right to know.*

Dogbert •641

*Journalism largely consists in saying 'Lord Jones Dead' to people who never knew that Lord Jones was alive.*

G.K. Chesterton, *The Wisdom of Father Brown (1914)* •642

*Journalists belong in the gutter because that is where the ruling classes throw their guilty secrets.*

Gerald Priestland, in *Observer 22 May 1988 'Sayings of the Week'* •643

*He who breaks this tablet or puts it
in water or rubs it until you cannot
recognize it [and] cannot make it be
understood, may Ashur, Sin, Shamash,
Adad and Ishtar, Bel, Nergal, Ishtar of
Nineveh, Ishtar of Arbela, Ishtar of Bit
Kidmurri, the gods of heaven and earth
and the gods of Assyria, may all these
curse him with a curse which cannot
be relieved, terrible and merciless, as
long a he lives, may they let his name,
his seed, be carried off from the land,
may they put his flesh in a dog's mouth!*

Inscription on a clay tablet found in the ruins
of a royal palace at Ashur, Assyria, 7th-3rd
century BC. In *Lionel Casson, Libraries of the
Ancient World (2001)* •644

*The human race, to which so
many of my readers belong.*

G.K. Chesterton, *The Napoleon
of Notting Hill (1904)* •645

¶

# THE SEVEN AGES OF MAN

All the world's a stage,
And all the men and women merely players,
They have their exits and entrances,
And one man in his time plays many parts,
His acts being seven ages. At first the infant,
Mewling and puking in the nurse's arms.
  Then the whining schoolboy, with his satchel
And shining morning face, creeping like a snail
Unwillingly to school. And then the lover,
Sighing like furnace, with a woeful ballad
Made to his mistress' eyebrow.
Then a soldier, Full of strange oaths and
  bearded like the pard,
Jealous in honour, sudden and quick in quarrel,
Seeking the bubble reputation
Even in the cannon's mouth. And then
  the justice,
In fair round belly with good capon lined,
With eyes severe and beard of formal cut,
Full of wise saws and modern instances;
And so he plays his part. The sixth age shifts
Into the lean and slippered pantaloon,
With spectacles on nose and pouch on side,
His youthful hose, well saved, a world too wide,
For his shrunk shank; and his big manly voice,
Turning again towards the childish treble, pipes
And whistles in his sound. Last scene of all,
That ends this strange eventful history,
  Is second childishness and mere oblivion,
Sans teeth, sans eyes, sans taste,
  sans everything.

**William Shakespeare,**
*As You Like It, (1599) II.vii* ▸646

*I wish either my father or my mother,
or indeed both of them, as they were
in duty both equally bound to it, had
minded what they were about when
they begot me.* Laurence Sterne,
*Tristram Shandy (1759-67)*
•649

# I s'pect I growed. Don't think nobody never made me.

Harriet Beecher Stowe, *Uncle Tom's Cabin
(1852) — said by Topsy* •650

*My mother groand! My father wept.
  Into the dangerous world I leapt:
Helpless, naked, piping loud:
  Like a fiend in a cloud.
Struggling in my father's hands:
  Striving against my swaddling bands:
Bound and weary I thought best
  To sulk upon my mother's breast.*

William Blake, *Songs of Experience (1794)* •647

## In the dark womb
  where I began
My mother's life made
  me a man

John Masefield, *'C.L.M', (1910)* •648

*A million million spermatozoa,
  All of them alive:
Out of their cataclysm but one
  poor Noah
Dare hope to survive,
And among that billion minus one
Might have chanced to be
Shakespeare, another Newton,
  a new Donne —
But the One was Me.*

Aldous Huxley, *Fifth
Philosopher's Song (1920)* •651

*Every baby born into the world is a finer one than the last.*

Charles Dickens,
*Nicholas Nickleby (1839)* •652

*Good work, Mary. We all knew you had it in you.*

Dorothy Parker, in *a letter to Mrs Mary Sherwood on the arrival of her baby. In Alexander Woollcott, While Rome Burns, 1934* •653

*Our birth is but a sleep and
 a forgetting…*

*Not in entire forgetfulness,*

*And not in utter nakedness,*

*But trailing clouds of glory
 do we come.*

William Wordsworth, *Ode: Intimations of Immortality (1807)* •654

*Love set you going like a
 fat gold watch.*

*The midwife slapped your footsoles,
 and your bald cry*

*Took its place among the elements.*

Sylvia Plath, *'Morning Song', (1966)* •655

*In every child who is born, under no matter what circumstances, and no matter what parents, the potentiality of the human race is born again.*

US novelist and poet James Agee, *Let Us Now Praise Famous Men (1931)* •656

*A bit of talcum
Is always walcum.*

Ogden Nash, *Free Wheeling (1931)* •657

¶

*Sweet childish days,
that were as long
As twenty days are now.*

William Wordsworth, *'To a Butterfly' (1807)* •658

*Behold the child, by Nature's
kindly law
Pleased with a rattle, tickled
with a straw.*

Alexander Pope, *An Essay on Man —
Epsitle 2 (1733)* •659

*Heaven lies
about us in
our infancy!*

William Wordsworth, *'Ode. Intimations
of Immortality' (1807)* •660

*Childhood is not from birth to a
  certain age and at a certain age*

*The child is grown, and puts away
  childish things.*

*Childhood is the kingdom where
  nobody dies.*

*Nobody that matters, that is.*

Edna St. Vincent Millay, *'Childhood is the
Kingdom where Nobody dies' (1934)* •661

*You are better than all the ballads,*
*That ever were sung or said;*
*For ye are living poems,*
*And all the rest are dead.*

Henry Wadsworth Longfellow, *'Children'* •664

*The Child is Father of the Man*

William Wordsworth, *'My heart leaps up
when I behold'* •662

*What music is
more enchanting
than the voices
of young people,
when you can't
hear what they
say?* Logan Pearsall Smith,
American essayist, *Afterthoughts
(1931) 'Age and Death'* •665

*A decrepit father
  takes delight*
*To see his active child
  do deeds of youth.*

William Shakespeare, *Sonnet 37* •663

*It should be noted that children at play are not merely playing; their games should be seen as their most serious actions.*

Montaigne, *Essais (1580)* •669

*Children sweeten labours, but they make misfortunes more bitter.*

Francis Bacon, *Essays (1625)* •666

*A child should always say
  what's true,
And speak when he is
  spoken to,
And behave mannerly at table:
At least as far as he is able.*

Robert Louis Stevenson, *A Child's Garden of Verses (1885)* •670

*The child that is not clean and neat,
With lots of toys and things to eat,
He is a naughty child, I'm sure —
Or else his dear papa is poor.*

Robert Louis Stevenson, *A Child's Garden of Verses (1885)* •668

*'Tis not good that children should know any wickedness.*

William Shakespeare, *The Merry Wives of Windsor (1597-8) II.ii* •671

It is only rarely that one can see in a little boy the promise of a man, but one can almost always see in a little girl the threat of a woman.

Alexandre Dumas (Fils); *attrib.* •672

The childhood shows the man,
As morning shows the day.

Milton, *Paradise Regained (1671) Book.4* •674

Anybody who has survived his childhood has enough information about life to last him the rest of his days.

Flannery O'Connor, in *New York Times Book Review, 1989* •673

There is always one moment in childhood when the door opens and lets the future in.

Graham Greene, *The Power and the Glory (1940)* •675

¶

*For the hand that rocks the cradle
Is the hand that rules the world.*

William Ross Wallace, *What Rules the World*
*(1865)* •676

*Children aren't happy
with nothing to ignore,
And that's what parents
were created for.*

Ogden Nash, *'The Parent', (1933)* •677

*Familiarity
breeds
contempt
— and
children.*

Mark Twain, *Notebooks (1935)* •678

*Childbirth was the moment of truth in my life. Suddenly you realise that you are having the greatest love affair of your life (but you also realise that God's a bloke).*

Australian novelist Kathy Lette,
in *The Observer* June 1999 •679

*What did my fingers do before
   they held him?*
*What did my heart do, with its love?*
*I have never seen a thing so clear.*
*His lids are like the lilac flower.*
*And soft as a moth, his breath.*
*I shall not let go.*
*There is no guile or warp in him.
   May he keep so.*

Sylvia Plath, on seeing her newborn baby;
'Three Women: A Poem for Three Voices' (1962) •680

*Claudia… remembered that when she'd had her first baby she had realised with astonishment that the perfect couple consisted of a mother and child and not, as she had always supposed, a man and woman.*

British writer Alice Thomas Ellis,
*The Other Side of the Fire (1983)* •681

*Who ran to help me when I fell,
And would some pretty story tell,
Or kiss the place to make it well?
My Mother.*

Ann Taylor and Jane Taylor,
'My Mother' (1804) •682

*Few misfortunes can befall a boy which bring worse consequences than having a really affectionate mother.*

W. Somerset Maugham, *A Writer's Notebook*,
written *1896*, pub. *1949* •683

*What do girls do when they haven't any mothers to help them through their troubles?*

Louisa May Alcott, *Little Women* (1868) •684

James James
Morrison Morrison
Weatherby George Dupree
Took great
Care of his Mother
Though he was only three.
James James
Said to his Mother,
'Mother,' he said, said he;
'You must never go down to the end
of the town, if you don't go down
with me'.

A.A. Milne, *When We Were Very Young,*
*(1924) 'Disobedience'* •685

*It is not that I half knew my mother. I knew half of her —
her lap, legs, feet, her hands and wrists as she bent forward.*

Flann O'Brien, *The Hard Life, (1961)* •686

*If I were damned of body and soul,
I know whose presence would
make me whole,
Mother o' mine, O mother o' mine.*

Rudyard Kipling, *'The Light That Failed' (1891)* •687

*So for the mother's sake
the child was dear,
And dearer was the
mother for the child.*

Coleridge, *'Sonnet to a Friend Who Asked
How I Felt When the Nurse First Presented
My Infant to Me' (1797)* •688

*I loved my parents (and I had more than the usual number to love).*

Quentin Bell, of his biological parents Clive and Vanessa Bell, and Duncan Grant (father of his half-sister); in *Daily Telegraph 18 December 1996;* obituary •689

*My wish was that my husband should be distinguished for intellect, and my children too. I have had my wish, — and I now wish that there was a little less intellect in the family so as to allow for a little more common sense.*

Frances Rossetti, mother to William, Christina and Dante Gabriel; in *William Rossetti (ed.) Dante Gabriel Rossetti: His Family Letters with a Memoir (1895)* •690

*A child is owed the greatest respect; if you ever have something disgraceful in mind, don't ignore your son's tender years.*

Juvenal, *Satires* •691

*It is a wise father that knows his own child.*

William Shakespeare, *The Merchant of Venice (1596-8) II.ii* •692

*Honour thy father and thy mother.*

Bible, *Exodus 20.12* •693

*I prithee, daughter, do not make me mad.*

William Shakespeare, *King Lear (1605-6) II.iv* •694

*A slavish bondage to parents cramps every faculty of the mind.*

Mary Wollstonecraft, *A Vindication of the Rights of Woman, (1792)* •696

*An unhappy alternative is before you, Elizabeth. From this day you must be a stranger to one of your parents. Your mother will never see you again if you do not marry Mr Collins, and I will never see you again if you do.*

Mr Bennet's finest moment, in Jane Austen's *Pride and Prejudice (1813)* •695

*A wise son maketh a glad father: but a foolish son is the heaviness of his mother.* Bible, Proverbs 10.1 •697

*He that spareth his rod hateth his son*

Bible, Proverbs 13.24 •698

Man hands on
 misery to man.
It deepens like a
 coastal shelf.
Get out as early
 as you can,
And don't have
 any kids yourself.

Philip Larkin, *This Be the Verse* 1974 •699

¶

*Girls scream,
Boys shout;
Dogs bark,
School's out.*

W.H. Davies, *'School's Out';*
published in *Collected Poems*
*(1963)* ·700

*The direction in
which education
starts a man will
determine his
future life.*

Plato ·701

*Education ent only books and music
— it's asking questions, all the time.*

Arnold Wesker, *Roots 1959* ·702

*Knowledge which is acquired
under compulsion has no hold
on the mind. Therefore do not
use compulsion, but let early
education be rather a sort of
amusement. This will better
enable you to find out the
natural bent of the child.*

Plato, with a sentiment shared by
schoolchildren everywhere. ·703

School's
Out

*The roots of education are bitter, but the fruit is sweet.*

Aristotle, in *Diogenes Laertius, Lives of Philosophers* •704

*It is no matter what you teach them [children] first, any more than what leg you shall put into your breeches first.*

Samuel Johnson, in *Boswell's Life of Samuel Johnson (1791) 26 July 1763* •705

*EDUCATION. — At Mr Wackford Squeer's Academy, Dotheboys Hall, at the delightful village of Dotheboys, near Greta Bridge in Yorkshire, Youth are boarded, clothed, booked, furnished with pocket-money, provided with all necessaries, instructed in all languages, living and dead, mathematics, orthography, geometry, trigonometry, the use of the globes, algebra, single stick (if required), writing, arithmetic, fortification, and every other branch of classical literature. Terms, twenty guineas per annum. No extras, no vacations, and diet unparalleled.*

Charles Dickens, *Nicholas Nickleby (1839)* •706

*We class schools, you see, into four grades: Leading school, First-rate School, Good school, and School. Frankly,' said Mr Levy, 'School is pretty bad.'*

Evelyn Waugh, *Decline and Fall (1928)* •707

*C-l-e-a-n, clean, verb active, to make bright, to scour. W-i-n, win, d-e-r, der, winder, a casement. When a boy knows this out of the book, he goes and does it.*

Charles Dickens, *Nicholas Nickleby (1839)* •708

*Ignorance is like a delicate exotic fruit; touch it and the bloom is gone. The whole theory of modern education is radically unsound. Fortunately, in England, at any rate, education produces no effect whatsoever.*

Oscar Wilde, *The Importance of Being Earnest (1895)* •709

*'I don't care a straw for Greek particle, or the digamma, no more does his mother. What is he sent to school for?… If he'll only turn out a brave, helpful, truth-telling Englishman, and a gentleman, and a Christian, that's all I want,' thought the Squire.*

Thomas Hughes, *Thomas Brown's Schooldays (1857)* •710

*I pay the schoolmaster, but 'tis the schoolboys that educate my son.*

Ralph Waldo Emerson, *Journals* •711

*For every person who wants to teach there are approximately thirty who don't want to learn — much.*

W.C. Sellar and R.J. Yeatman, *And Now All This (1932)* •712

*Someone once said, Rumbold, that education is what is left when you have forgotten all that you have ever learned. You appear to be trying to circumvent the process by learning as little as possible.* Alan Bennett,

*Forty Years On (1969)* •713

'That's the reason they're called lessons,' the Gryphon remarked: 'because they lessen from day to day.' **Lewis Carroll**, *Alice's Adventures in Wonderland (1865)* •714

Multiplication is vexation,
Division is as bad;
The Rule of Three doth
  puzzle me,
And Practice drives me mad.

**Anonymous**, *Lean's Collectanea vol.4 (1904); possibly 16th-century* •715

The only good things about skool are the BOYS WIZZ who are noble brave fearless etc. although you hav various swots, bulies, cissies, milksops, greedy guts and oiks with whom i am forced to mingle hem-hem.

**Geoffrey Willans and Ronald Searle**, *Down With Skool! (1953)* •716

Alas, regardless of their doom,
The little victims play!
No sense have they of ills to come,
Nor care beyond a day

**Thomas Gray**, *'Ode on a Distant Prospect of Eton College' (1747)* •717

# The scholar who cherishes the love of comfort, is not fit to be deemed a scholar.

**Confucius**, *Analects* •718

There is now less flogging in our great schools than formerly, but then less is learned there; so what the boys get at one end they lose at the other.

**Samuel Johnson, in** *James Boswell, Life of Samuel Johnson (1791) 1775* •719

*The dread of beatings!
Dread of being late!*

*And, greatest dread of all,
the dread of games!*

John Betjeman,
*'Summoned by Bells' (1960)* •720

*Public schools are
the nurseries of all
vice and immorality.*

Henry Fielding, *Joseph Andrews (1742)* •722

*He must have known
me had he seen me
as he was wont to see
me, for he was in the
habit of flogging me
constantly. Perhaps
he did not recognize
me by my face.*

Anthony Trollope, of his headmaster,
*Autobiography (1883)* •721

*Good gracious, you've
got to educate him first.
You can't expect a boy
to be vicious till he's
been to a good school.*

Saki, *Reginald in Russia (1910)* •723

¶

*Dost thou think, because thou art virtuous, that there shall be no more cakes and ale?*

William Shakespeare,
*Twelfth Night (1601) II.iii* •724

# *It is better to waste one's youth than to do nothing with it at all.*

Georges Courteline, French dramatist and novelist, *La Philosophie de Georges Courteline (1948)* •725

*I would there were no age between ten and three-and-twenty, or that youth would sleep out the rest; for there is nothing in the between but getting wenches with child, wronging the ancientry, stealing, fighting.*

William Shakespeare,
*The Winter's Tale III.iii* •726

*The young always have the same problem — how to rebel and conform at the same time. They have now solved this by defying their parents and copying one another.*

Quentin Crisp, *The Naked Civil Servant.* •727

*Undergraduates owe their chief happiness to the consciousness that they are no longer at school. The nonsense which was knocked out of them at school is all put gently back into them at Oxford or Cambridge.* Max Beerbohm, *More (1899)* •728

*Let schoolmasters puzzle their brain,*
*With grammar, and nonsense, and learning,*
*Good liquor, I stoutly maintain,*
*Gives genius a better discerning.*
Oliver Goldsmith, *She Stoops to Conquer (1773)* •730

*The exquisite art of idleness, one of the most important things that any university can teach.*
Oscar Wilde •729

*It was remarked to me… that to play billiards well was a sign of an ill-spent youth.*
English philosopher and journalist Herbert Spencer, in *Duncan, Life and Letters of Spencer (1908)* •731

*If I had no duties, and no reference to futurity, I would spend my life in driving briskly in a post-chaise with a pretty woman.*
Samuel Johnson, in *Boswell, Life of Samuel Johnson (1791), 19 September 1777* •732

*Cheerfulness gives elasticity to the spirit. Spectres fly before it.*

Samuel Smiles, *Self-Help (1859)* •733

*It would be mortifying to the feelings of many ladies, could they be made to understand how little the heart of man is affected by what is costly or new in their attire.*

Jane Austen, *Northanger Abbey (1818)* •734

*Live all you can; it's a mistake not to. It doesn't so much matter what you do in particular, so long as you have your life. If you haven't had that, what have you had?* Henry James, *The Ambassadors (1903)* •735

*One cannot have too large a party. A large party secures its own amusement.* Jane Austen, *Emma (1816)* •736

*All the adaptations I saw before were with people in stiff suits standing up very straight making polite conversation through pursed lips in drawing rooms. But I felt the story is more about young men and women in the prime of their lives with lots of hormones pounding around.*

Andrew Davies on *Pride and Prejudice,* which he adapted for the BBC. Speaking at Banff Television Festival *1999* •737

*A merry heart doeth good like a medicine.*

Bible, Proverbs 17:22 •738

*A cigarette is the perfect type of a perfect pleasure. It is exquisite and leaves one quiet unsatisfied. What more can one want?*

Oscar Wilde •740

*A man hath no better thing under the sun, than to eat, and to drink, and to be merry.*

Bible, Ecclessiastes 8:15 •739

*The road of excess leads to the palace of wisdom.*

William Blake, *The Marriage of Heaven and Hell (1790-93)* •741

*LSD? Nothing much happened, but I did get the distinct impression that some birds were trying to communicate with me.*

W.H. Auden, in *George Plimpton (ed.), The Writer's Chapbook (1989)* •742

*Man, being reasonable, must get drunk;*
*The best of life is but intoxication.*

Lord Byron, *Don Juan (1819-24)* •743

# Gin-and-water is the source of all my inspiration.

Lord Byron, *Conversations (1824)* •746

*What does drunkenness not accomplish? It unlocks secrets, confirms our hopes, urges the indolent into battle, lifts the burden from anxious minds, teaches new arts.*

Horace •744

# We'll drink one another's healths, and spoil our own.

Jerome K. Jerome, *Idle Thoughts of an Idle Fellow (1889)* •747

*And malt does more than Milton can*
*To justify God's ways to man.*
*Ale, man, ale's the stuff to drink*
*For fellows whom it hurts to think.*

A.E. Housman, *A Shropshire Lad (1896)* •745

*Wine leads to folly. It makes even the wisest laugh too much. It makes him dance. It makes him say what should have been left unsaid.*

Homer ·748

**Breslin's Rule:** *Don't trust a brilliant idea unless it survives a hangover.*

Jimmy Breslin ·749

*Let us have wine and women, mirth and laughter,*

*Sermons and soda-water the day after.*

Lord Byron, *Don Juan (1819-24)* ·750

*After the first glass of absinthe, you see things as you wish they were. After the second, you see them as they are not. Finally, you see things as they really are and that is the most horrible thing in the world.*

Oscar Wilde ·751

*I remember my youth and the feeling that will never come back any more — the feeling that I could last forever, outlast the sea, the earth, and all men*

Joseph Conrad, *Youth* ·752

*My salad days,*
*When I was green in judgement.*

William Shakespeare,
*Anthony and Cleopatra (1606-7) I.v* •753

*To find a young fellow that is*
*neither a wit in his own eye,*
*nor a fool in the eye of the*
*world, is a very hard task.*

William Congreve, *Love for Love (1695)* •754

*Of all the horrid, hideous*
  *notes of woe,*
*Sadder than owl-songs*
  *or the midnight blast,*
*Is that portentous phrase,*
  *'I told you so'.*

Lord Byron, *Don Juan (1819-24)* •755

¶

*The devil's most devilish when respectable.*

Elizabeth Barrett Browning,
*Aurora Leigh (1857)* •756

*At twenty years of age, the will reigns; at thirty, the wit; and at forty, the judgement.*

Benjamin Franklin, *Poor Richard's Almanac (1741)* •758

*Nel mezzo del cammin di nostra vita. — Midway along the path of our life.*

Dante Alighieri *1265-1321, Divina Commedia, 'Inferno'* •757

*...when I became a man I put away, I put away childish things.*

Bible, I Corinthians 13.1 •759

When I was ten, I read fairy tales in secret, and would have been ashamed of being found doing so. Now that I am fifty, I read them openly. When I became a man, I put away childish things, including the fear of childishness and the desire to be very grown up.

**C.S. Lewis,** *'On Three Ways of Writing for Children' (1952)* •760

There is no good end attained by trying to persuade ourselves that women are all incorporeal, angelic, colourless, passionless, helpless creatures…Women have especial need, as the world goes, to be shrewd, self-reliant, and strong; and we do all we can in our literature to render them helpless, imbecile, and idiotic.

**Justin McCarthy,** in *Westminster Review 1864* •763

Be wise with speed;
A fool at forty is a fool indeed.

**Edward Young,** *'The Love of Fame' (1725-8)* •761

It is no use telling me that there are bad aunts and good aunts. At the core they are all alike. Sooner or later, out pops the cloven hoof.

**P.G. Wodehouse,** *The Code of the Woosters* •764

One of the pleasures of middle age is to find out  that one WAS right, and that one was much righter than one knew at say 17 or 23.

**Ezra Pound,** *ABC of Reading (1934)* •762

*Mrs Badcock and two young women were of the same party, except when Mrs Badcock thought herself obliged to leave them to run around the room after her drunken husband. His avoidance, and her pursuit, with the probable intoxication of both, was an amusing scene.*

**Jane Austen**, *Letter to her sister, Cassandra* ·765

*All happy families resemble one another, but each unhappy family is unhappy in its own way.* Leo Tolstoy, *Anna Karenina (1875-77)*

·766

*Good breeding consists in concealing how much we think of ourselves and how little we think of other persons.*

**Mark Twain**, *Notebook, 1935* ·767

*Every idiot who goes about with Merry Christmas on his lips should be boiled with his own pudding, and buried with a stake of holly through his heart.*

**Charles Dickens**, *A Christmas Carol (1843)* ·768

*A servant's too often a negligent elf;*
*— If it's business of consequence,*
*DO IT YOURSELF!*

**R. H. Barham**, *'The Ingoldsby Penence!*
*— Moral' (1842)* ·769

*You think that I am cruel and gluttonous when I beat my cook for sending in a bad dinner. But if that is too trivial a cause, what other can there be for beating a cook?* Martial •770

# More childish valorous than manly wise.

Christopher Marlowe,
*Tamburlaine the Great (1590)* •771

## To his dog, every man is Napoleon; hence the constant popularity of dogs.

Aldous Huxley •772

*The proper office of a friend is to side with you when you are in the wrong. Nearly anybody will side with you when you are in the right.* Mark Twain,
*Notebooks, 1935* •773

*It's no good trying to keep up old friendships. It's painful for both sides. The fact is, one grows out of people, and the only thing is to face it.*

Novelist and short-story writer
W. Somerset Maugham,
*Cakes and Ale, 1930.* •774

The heart may think it knows better: the senses know absence blots people out. We have really no absent friends.

Anglo-Irish novelist and short-story writer
Elizabeth Bowen, *Death of the Heart, 1938* •775

It is better to be beautiful than to be good. But… it is better to be good than to be ugly.

Oscar Wilde, *The Picture of Dorian Gray (1891)* •776

The flowers anew, returning seasons bring;
But beauty faded has no second spring.

Ambrose Philips, *The First Pastoral (1708)* •777

I am resolved to grow fat and look young till forty, and then slip out of the world with the first wrinkle and the reputation of five-and-twenty.

John Dryden, *The Maiden Queen (1668)* •778

Rough winds do shake the darling buds of May,
And summer's lease hath all too short a date.

William Shakespeare, *Sonnet 18* •779

*We have followed too much the devices and desires of our own hearts.*

*The Book of Common Prayer (1662), Morning Prayer General Confession* •780

*Up, and at my chamber all morning in the office, doing business and also reading a little of L'escolle des Filles, which is a mighty lewd book, but yet not amiss for a sober man once read over to inform himself in the villainy of the world.*

**Samuel Pepys,** *Diary 1668.* **Sober man indeed — that's what they all say** •781

*I don't like baths, I don't enjoy them in the slightest and, if I could, I'd prefer to go around dirty.*

**J.B. Priestley,** *Observer, 1979* •782

*The truth is, that in London it is always a sickly season. Nobody is healthy in London, nobody can be.*

**Jane Austen, Mr Woodhouse in** *Emma (1816)* •783

*My life is one demd horrid grind!*

**Charles Dickens,** *Nicholas Nickleby (1839)* •784

*Success is relative:*
*It is what we can make of the*
*mess we have made of things.*

**T.S. Eliot**, *The Family Reunion (1939)* ·787

*I refuse to endure months of*
*expensive humiliation only to be*
*told that at the age of four I was*
*in love with my rocking-horse.*

Noël Coward on 'therapy' ·785

# Every man has a lurking wish to appear considerable in his native place.

Samuel Johnson, *letter to Joshua Reynolds, 17 July 1771* ·788

## He was meddling too much in my private life.

Tennessee Williams on why he had given up visiting his psychoanalyst ·786

*If you would not be forgotten*
*as soon as you are dead, either*
*write things worth reading or*
*do things worth writing.*

US statesman Benjamin Franklin, *attrib.* ·789

They are not long, the days
  of wine and roses:
Out of a misty dream
Our path emerges for a while,
  then closes
Within a dream.

Ernest Dowson, 'Vitae Summa Brevis' (1896) •790

We wove a web in childhood,
A web of sunny air;
We dug a spring in infancy
Of water pure and fair;
We sowed in youth a mustard seed,
We cut an almond rod;
We are now grown to riper age —
Are they withered in the sod?

Charlotte Brontë, 'We wove a web in childhood'
(written 1835) •791

As they say, when the
age is in, the wit is out.

William Shakespeare, Much Ado
About Nothing III.v (1598) •792

I have a bone to pick with Fate,
Come here and tell me, girlie,
Do you think my mind is
  maturing late,
Or simply rotted early?

Ogden Nash, 'Lines on Facing Forty' (1942) •793

No arts; no letters; no
society; and which is worst
of all, continual fear and
danger of violent death;
and the life of man,
solitary, poor, nasty,
brutish, and short.

Thomas Hobbes,
Leviathan (1651) •794

But at my back I always hear
Time's wingèd chariots hurrying near:
And yonder all before us lie
Deserts of vast eternity.

Andrew Marvell, *'To His Coy Mistress' (1681)* ·795

At thirty a man suspects
  himself a fool;
Knows it at forty, and reforms
  his plan;
at fifty chides his infamous
  delay,
Pushes his prudent purpose
  to resolve;
In all the magnaminity
  of thought
Resolves; and re-resolves;
  then dies the same.

Edward Young, *Night Thoughts (1742-45)* ·796

*We had the experience but missed the meaning.*

T.S. Eliot, *Four Quartets, 'The Dry Salvages' (1941)* ·797

¶

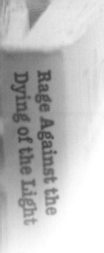

*I grow old... I grow old...*
*I shall wear the bottoms of*
*  my trousers rolled.*

**T.S. Eliot,** *'The Love Song of*
*J. Alfred Prufrock' (1917)* •799

## No one is so old that he does not think he could live another year.

**Roman orator and statesman Cicero,**
*De Senectute, 44 BC.* •800

*Do not go gentle in to that good night,*

*Old age should burn and rave at close*
*of day; Rage, rage against the dying*
*of the light.*

**Dylan Thomas,** *'Do Not Go Gentle into*
*that Good Night' (1952)* •798

*Gather ye rosebuds while ye may,*
*Old Time is still a-flying; and this*
*same flower that smiles today*
*tomorrow will be dying.*

**Robert Herrick,** *(1591-1674)* •801

*It is better to be seventy years young than forty years old!*

Oliver Wendell Holmes, in reply to an invitation from Julia Ward Howe to her seventieth birthday party, *27 May 1889* •804

*We talked about growing
  old gracefully*

*And Elsie, who's seventy-four,*

*Said, 'A, it's a question of being
  sincere, and*

*B, if you're supple you've
  nothing to fear.'*

*Then she swung upside down
  from a glass chandelier.*

*I couldn't have liked it more.*

Noël Coward, *I've been to a Marvellous Party*. Set to music, *1938* •805

*Is not old wine wholesomest, old pippins toothsomest, old wood burn brightest, old linen wash whitest Old soldiers, sweethearts, are surest, and old lovers are soundest.*

John Webster, *Westward Hoe (1607)* •802

*Age does not make us childish,
  as men tell*

*It merely finds us children
  still at heart.*

Johann Wolfgang von Goethe, *Faust pt.1 (1808)* •803

# *Though I look old, I am strong and lusty*

William Shakespeare, *As You Like It (1599)* •806

*No spring, nor summer beauty hath such grace, as I have seen in one autumnal face.*

Poet and divine John Donne,
'The Autumnal', Elegy 9, (1634) •807

*How happy he who crowns in shades like these,*

*A youth of labour with an age of ease.*

Oliver Goldsmith, *The Deserted Village (1770)* •810

*No pleasure is worth giving up for the sake of two more years in a geriatric home in Weston-super-Mare.*

Kingsley Amis, in *The Times*
*21 June 1994 (attrib.)* •808

*As you are old and reverend, you should be wise.*

William Shakespeare, *King Lear (1605-06) I.iv* •811

*The oldest hath borne most: we that are young, shall never see so much, nor live so long.*

William Shakespeare, *King Lear (1605-6) V.iii* •812

*Grow old along with me! The best is yet to be.*

Robert Browning,
'Rabbi Ben Ezra' (1864) •809

From the earliest times the old have rubbed it into the young that they are wiser than they, and before the young had discovered what nonsense this was they were old too, and it profited them to carry on the imposture. W. Somerset Maugham, *Cakes and Ale (1930)* •813

Age is deformed, youth unkind,
We scorn their bodies, they our mind.
Thomas Bastard, *Chrestoleros (1598)* •815

*W'en folks git ole en strucken wid de palsy, dey mus speck ter be laff'd at.*

Joel Chandler Harris, *Nights with Uncle Remus (1883)* •814

All that I have said and done,
Now that I am old and ill,
Turns into a question till
I lie awake night after night
And never get the answers right.
W.B. Yeats, *'The Man and the Echo' (1939)* •816

See how old age its
  veterans rewards!
A youth of frolics,
  an old age of cards.

Alexander Pope, *Epistles to Several Persons 'To a Lady' (1735)* •817

When you are old and
grey and full of sleep,
And nodding by the fire,
take down this book
And slowly read and
dream of the soft look
Your eyes had once, and
of their shadows deep.

W.B. Yeats, *'When You Are Old' (1893)* •818

What are those blue
remembered hills,
What spires, what
farms are those?
That is the land of
lost content,
I see it shining plain,
The happy highways
where I went
And cannot
come again.

A.E. Houseman, *A Shropshire Lad (1896)* •819

I have had playmates,
  I have had companions,

In my days of childhood, in
  my joyful school-days —

All, all are gone, the
  old familiar faces.

Charles Lamb *1775-1834*,
*'The Old Familiar Faces'* •820

How often are we to die before
we go quite off this stage? In
every friend we lose a part of
ourselves, and the best part.

Alexander Pope, *letter to Jonathan Swift,*
*5 December 1732* •821

Senescence begins and
  middle age ends

The day your descendants
  outnumber your friends.

Ogden Nash, *'Crossing the Border',*
*You Can't Get There from Here, (1957)* •822

And so, from hour to hour,
  we ripe and ripe,

And then, from hour to hour,
  we rot and rot:

And thereby hangs a tale.

William Shakespeare,
As You Like It (1599) II.vii •825

Even such is time, which takes in trust
Our youth, our joys, and all we have,
And pays us but with age and dust.

Walter Ralegh, written the night before
his death in 1618 •823

The days of our age are threescore
years and ten; and though men be
so strong that they come to fourscore
years: yet is their strength then but
labour and sorrow; so soon passeth
it away, and we are gone.

Bible, Psalm 90 •826

*Every man desires
to live long; but no
man would be old.*

Jonathan Swift, Thoughts on
Various Subjects (1727 ed.) •824

*I wasted time, and now
doth time waste me.*

William Shakespeare, Richard II (1595) V.v •827

*Though nothing can bring
  back the hour*

*Of splendour in the grass,
  of glory in the flower;*

*We will grieve not,
  rather find*

*Strength in what
  remains behind..*

*In the faith that looks
  through death,*

*In years that bring the
  philosophic mind.*

William Wordsworth, *'Ode.
Intimations of Immortality' (1807)* •828

*And almost every one when age,
Disease, or sorrows strike him,
Inclines to think there is a God,
Or something very like Him.*

Arthur Hugh Clough, *'Dipsychus' (1865)* •829

*For when the One Great Scorer*
  *comes to mark against your name,*
*He marks — not that you won or lost*
  *— but how you played the Game.*

US writer Grantland Rice,
*'Alumnus Football' (1941)* •830

¶

# *LOVE & LUST*

*Oh, what a dear ravishing thing
is the beginning of an Amour!*

**Aphra Behn,** *The Emperor of the Moon (1687)* ·831

L'Amour

Love sought is good, but giv'n unsought is better.

William Shakespeare,
*Twelfth Night (1601) III.i* •834

*In the spring a young man's fancy lightly turns to thoughts of love.*

Alfred, Lord Tennyson,
*'Locksley Hall' (1842)* •832

Love is the irresistible desire to be irresistibly desired. Robert Frost •835

*O! How this spring of love resembleth
The uncertain glory of an April day.*

William Shakespeare, *Two Gentlemen of Verona
(1592-3) I.iii* •833

*Drink to me only with thine eyes, and I will pledge with mine, or leave a kiss upon the cup, and I'll not look for wine.*

Playwright and poet Ben Jonson,
*'To Celia', 1616* •836

*Love is the wisdom of the fool and the folly of the wise.*

Samuel Johnson, in *William Cooke, Life of Samuel Foote (1805)* •837

*The lunatic, the lover, and the poet, Are of imagination all compact.*

William Shakespeare, *A Midummer Night's Dream (1595-6) V.i* •838

*My love for Linton is like the foliage in the woods; time will change it, I'm well aware, as winter changes the trees — My love for Heathcliff resembles the eternal rocks beneath: — a source of little visible delight, but necessary.* Emily Brontë, *Wuthering Heights (1847)* •839

*I will be horribly in love with her.*

Benedick of the equally scornful Beatrice, in William Shakespeare's *Much Ado About Nothing II.iii (1598)* •840

*The heart has its reasons which reason knows nothing of.*

Blaise Pascal, *Pensees (1670)* •841

*The speaking in perpetual hyperbole is comely in nothing but in love*

Francis Bacon, *Essays (1625) 'Of Love'* •842

*O wonderful, wonderful, and most wonderful wonderful! And yet again wonderful, and after that, out of all whooping!*

William Shakespeare, *As You Like It* (1599) III.ii •843

## Can he wel speke of love? quod she

Geoffrey Chaucer, *Troilus and Criseyde, Book II* •844

*I'll love you, dear, I'll love you
Till China and Africa meet
And the river jumps over the mountain
And the salmon sing in the street,
I'll love you till the ocean
Is folded and hung up to dry
And the seven stars go squawking
Like geese about the sky.*

W.H. Auden, *'As I Walked Out One Evening'* (1940) •846

*All a lovers' wish can reach
For the joy my love shall teach
And for thy Pleasure shall improve
All that Art can add to love.
Yet still I love thee without Art,
Ancient person of my heart.*

Courtier and poet John Wilmot, Earl of Rochester, *'A Song of a Young Lady to her Ancient Lover'* •845

## And she was as fayr as is the rose in May.

Geoffrey Chaucer, *The Legend of Good Women, 'Cleopatra'* •847

*O, she doth teach the torches to burn bright!*

William Shakespeare, *Romeo and Juliet,* *(1595)* I.v •848

*Pains of love be sweeter far than all other pleasures are.*

Poet and playwright John Dryden, *Tyrannic Love, 1669* •851

*O, my Luve's like a red, red rose
That's newly sprung in June;
O my Luve's like the melodie
That's sweetly play'd in tune.*

Robert Burns, *'A Red Red Rose' (1796),* derived from various folk songs •849

*Love is not love
Which alters when it alteration finds.*

William Shakespeare, *Sonnet 116* •852

*She knows her man, and when you rant and swear, Can draw you to her with a single hair.*

John Dryden, translation of *Persius Satires* •850

*My true love hath my heart and I have his,*

*By just exchange one for the other giv'n;*

*I hold his dear, and mine he cannot miss,*

*There never was a better bargain driv'n.*

Philip Sidney, *Arcadia (1581)* •853

To love is to admire with the heart; to admire is to love with the mind.

French man of letters Theophile Gautier •854

How do I love thee? Let me count the ways. I love thee to the depth and breadth and height My soul can reach.

Poet Elizabeth Barrett Browning
'Sonnets from the Portuguese'. No. 43, 1850 •855

What I have done is yours; what I have to do is yours; being part in all I have, devoted yours.

William Shakespeare,
The Rape of Lucrece (1595) •856

To say a man is fallen in love, — or that he is deeply in love, — or up to the ears in love, — and sometimes even head over heels in it, — carries an idiomatical kind of implication, that love is a thing below a man.

Laurence Sterne, Tristram Shandy 1759-67 •857

Love has no other desire but to fulfil itself.

Syrian writer and artist Kahlil Gibran,
The Prophet, 1923 •858

*What is love? 'tis not hereafter;*
*Present mirth hath present laughter;*
*What's to come is still unsure:*
*In delay there lies no plenty;*
*Then come kiss me, sweet and twenty,*
*Youth's a stuff will not endure.*

William Shakespeare, *Twelfth Night, II. ii (1601)* •859

*Where do the noses go? I always wondered where the noses would go.*

Ernest Hemingway, *For Whom the Bell Tolls (1940)* •860

*This wondrous miracle did Love devise,*
*For dancing is love's proper exercise.*

John Davies, *'Orchestra, or a Poem of Dancing' (1596)* •861

*All the privilege I claim for my own sex... is that of loving longest, when existence or when hope is gone.*

Jane Austen, *Persuasion, (1818)* •862

*One word frees us from all the weight and pain of life. That word is love.*

Sophocles •863

*Give me my Romeo; and, when he shall die, take him and cut him out in little stars, and he will make the face of heaven so fine that all the world will be in love with night and pay no worship to the garish sun.*

William Shakespeare, *Romeo and Juliet, (1595) III.ii* •864

# The magic of first love is our ignorance that it can ever end.

Benjamin Disreali, *Henrietta Temple (1837)* •865

*I wish you could invent some means to make me at all happy without you. Every hour I am more and more concentrated in you; everything else tastes like chaff in my mouth.*

John Keats, *letter to Fanny Brawne, August 1820* •866

I hold it true, whate'er befall; I feel it, when I sorrow most; 'Tis better to have loved and lost than never to have loved at all.

Poet Lord Tennyson, *In Memoriam A.H.H., (1850), Canto 28* •867

He was my North,
my South, my East,
my West,
My working week
and my Sunday rest,
My noon, my midnight,
my talk, my song;
I thought that love
would last for ever.
I was wrong.

W.H. Auden, *Funeral Blues*,
originally in the play
*The Ascent of F6* 1937 •868

Though they go mad they
shall be sane,
Though they sink through the
sea they shall rise again;
Though lovers be lost,
love shall not;
And death shall have
no dominion.

Welsh poet and writer Dylan Thomas,
'And Death Shall Have No Dominion', 1936 •869

Take away love and
our earth is a tomb.

Poet Robert Browning •870

Omnia vincit Amor: et nos cedamus
Amori. — Love conquers all things:
let us too give in to Love.

Virgil, *Eclogues* •871

*She was the beat of my heart for thirty years. She was the music heard faintly on the edge of sound. It was my great and now useless regret that I never wrote anything really worth her attention, no book that I could dedicate to her. I planned it. I thought of it, but I never wrote it. Perhaps I couldn't have written it.*

Raymond Chandler after the death of his wife, *letter to Leonard Russell, 29 December 1954* •872

¶

Reader, I married him.

Charlotte Brontë, *Jane Eyre (1847)* •873

Marriage is the greatest earthly happiness when founded on complete sympathy. Benjamin Disreali, *letter to Gladstone* •875

Flesh of Flesh,

Bone of my One thou art, and from thy State,

Mine shall never be parted, weal or woe.

John Milton, *Paradise Lost (1667)* •874

I sing of brooks, of blossoms, birds, and bowers:
Of April, May, of June and July-flowers.
I sing of May-poles, wassails, wakes,
Of bride-grooms, brides, and of their bridal-cakes.

Robert Herrick, *'The Argument of his Book' from Hesperides (1648)* •876

*The joys of marriage are
  the heaven on earth,
Life's paradise, great princess,
  the soul's quiet.*

John Ford, *The Broken Heart (1633) II.ii* •877

*Love seems the swiftest but it is
the slowest of all growths. No man
or woman really knows what a
perfect love is until they have been
married a quarter of a century.*

Mark Twain, *Notebook 1894* •878

*People talk about beautiful friendships between
two persons of the same sex. What is the best
of that sort, as compared with the friendship
of man and wife, where the best impulses and
highest ideals of both are the same? There is
no place for comparison between the two
friendships; the one is earthly, the other divine.*

Mark Twain, *A Connecticut Yankee (1889)* •879

*What a happy and holy fashion it is
that those who love one another
should rest on the same pillow.*

Nathaniel Hawthorne •880

*Opening her eyes
again, and seeing her
husband's face across
the table, she leaned
forward to give it a
pat on the cheek, and
sat down to supper,
declaring it to be the
best face in the world.*

Charles Dickens, *Our Mutual Friend (1865)* •881

*The quiet mutual gaze of a trusting husband and wife is like the first moment of rest or refuge from a great weariness or a great danger.*

George Eliot, *Silas Marner (1861)* •882

*And at home by the fire, whenever you look up, there I shall be — and whenever I look up there you will be.*

Thomas Hardy, *Far from the Madding Crowd (1874)*. **Gabriel Oak proposing to Bathsheba Everdene.** •883

*She is a woman, therefore may be wooed;*

*She is a woman, therefore may be won.*

William Shakespeare, *Titus Andronicus (1590) II.i* •884

*A lady's imagination is very rapid; it jumps from admiration to love, from love to matrimony in a moment.* Jane Austen, **Mr Darcy** in *Pride and Prejudice (1813)* •885s

*I never had one hour's happiness in her society, and yet my mind all round the four-and-twenty hours was harping on the happiness of having her with me unto death.*

Charles Dickens, *Great Expectations (1861)* •886

Mr Richard Harvey is going to be married; but as it is a great secret and only known to half the neighbourhood, you must not mention it.

**Jane Austen**, *Letter to her sister, Cassandra* •887

---

**Miranda:** *My husband then?*
**Ferdinand:** *Ay, with a heart as willing*
*As bondage e'er of freedom.*

**William Shakespeare**, *The Tempest (1611) III.i* •888

Being a husband is a whole-time job. That is why so many husbands fail at it. They cannot give their entire attention to it.

**Arnold Bennett**, *The Title (1918) Act 1* •890

'My lige lady, generally,' quod he,
'Wommen desiren to have
    sovereynetee
As wel over hir housbond as
    hir love'.

**Geoffrey Chaucer**, *The Canterbury Tales, 'Wife of Bath's Tale'* •889

*If you are afraid of loneliness, don't marry.*

**Anton Chekhov** •891

*Marriage has many pains, but celibacy has no pleasures.*

Samuel Johnson, *Rasselas, (1759)* •892

*You shall be together when the white wings of death scatter your days. Ay, you shall be together even in the silent memory of God. But let there be spaces in your togetherness, and let the winds of the heavens dance between you.*

Syrian writer and artist Kahlil Gibran, *'On Marriage', in the Prophet, (1923)* •893

*The sum which two married people owe to one another defies calculation. It is an infinite debt, which can only be discharged through eternity.*

Johann Wolfgang von Goethe •894

¶

*In her first passion woman loves her lover, in all the others all she loves is love.*

Lord Byron, *Don Juan, 1819-24* •897

*Of soup and love, the first is the best.*

Thomas Fuller, *Gnomologia (1732)* •895

*A good uniform must work its way with the women, sooner or later.*

Charles Dickens, *Pickwick Papers (1837)* •898

*Ay me! for aught that ever I could read,*

*could ever hear by tale or history,*

*the course of true love never did run smooth.*

William Shakespeare, *A Midsummer Night's Dream, (1595-6) I.i* •896

*My only books Were woman's looks, And folly's all they've taught me*

Thomas Moore, *'The time I've lost in wooing' 1807* •899

*Judgement of beauty can err, what with the wine and the dark.*

Ovid knows all about beer goggles ·900

*Keep you in the rear of your affection,
Out of the shot and danger of desire.*

William Shakespeare, *Hamlet (1601) I.iii*
— Laertes advises his sister Ophelia ·901

*Affection is a coal that
    must be cool'd;
Else, sufer'd, it will set
    the heart on fire.*

William Shakespeare,
*Venus and Adonis,(1593)
stanza 65* ·902

*Someone asked Sophocles, 'How is
your sex-life now? Are you still able to
have a woman?' He replied, 'Hush,
man; most gladly am I rid of it all, as
though I had escaped from a mad and
savage master.'*

Sophocles *(in Plato's Republic)*. ·903

*Love is just a dirty trick on us to achieve the continuation of the species.*

W. Somerset Maugham,
*A Writers Notebook, 1949* ·904

*Love built on beauty, soon as beauty, dies.*

John Donne, *Elegies 'The Anagram' (c.1595)* ·905

No one would ever have fallen in love unless he had first read about it.

Duc de la Rochefoucauld, in *Edmund White, The Burning Library (1994); attrib.* •906

Love is a grave mental disease.

Plato •908

I have met women whom I really think would like to be married to a poem and to be given away by a novel.

John Keats, *letter to Fanny Brawne, 8 July 1819* •907

My heart is a lonely hunter that hunts on a lonely hill.

Fiona McLeod, *'The Lonely Hunter' (1896)* •909

Love is like any other luxury. You have no right to it unless you can afford it.

Anthony Trollope, *The Way We Live Now (1875)* •910

*It is a truth universally acknowledged, that a single man in possession of a good fortune, must be in want of a wife.*

Jane Austen, *Pride and Prejudice* •911

*It would be an excellent match, for he was rich, and she was handsome.*

Jane Austen, *Sense and Sensibility (1811)* •912

*Love and a cottage! Eh, Fanny! Ah, give me indifference and a coach and six!*

George Colman, the Elder, and David Garrick, *The Clandestine Marriage (1766)* •913

*Oh, life is a glorious cycle of song,*

*A medley of extemporanea;*

*And love is a thing that can never go wrong;*

*And I am Marie of Roumania.*

Dorothy Parker, *'Comment' (1937)* •914

*It was a blonde. A blonde to make a bishop kick a hole in a stained glass window.* American detective fiction writer Raymond Chandler, *Farewell My Lovely, (1940)* •915

*Personal beauty is a greater recommendation than any letter of reference.*

Aristotle •916

*And what is bettre than wisedoom? Womman. And what is bettre than a good womman? Nothyng.*

Chaucer, *The Canterbury Tales, 'The Tale of Melibee'* •917

*Ful smale ypulled were hire browes two, And tho were bent and blake as any sloo. — (She'd thinned out carefully her eyebrows two, And they were arched and black as any sloe)*

Geoffrey Chaucer, *The Canterbury Tales, 'The Miller's Tale'* •918

*That's the thing about girls. Every time they do something pretty, even if they're not much to look at, or even if they're sort of stupid, you fall half in love with them and then you never know where the hell you are. Girls. Jesus Christ. They can drive you crazy, they really can.*

J.D. Salinger, *The Catcher in the Rye, (1951)* •919

The 'It' Factor

*Tisn't beauty, so to speak, nor good talk necessarily. It's just It. Some women'll stay in a man's memory if they once walked down a street.*

Rudyard Kipling, *Travels and Discoveries* (1904) •920

*She just wore Enough for modesty — no more.*

Robert Buchanan *'White Rose and Red'* (1873) •921

*It is very often nothing but our own vanity that deceives us. Women fancy admiration means more than it does.* Jane Austen, Jane Bennet in *Pride and Prejudice* (1813) •922

*Chastity — the most unnatural of all sexual perversions.* Aldous Huxley, *Eyeless in Gaza* (1936) •923

*Sexual intercourse began In nineteen sixty-three (Which was rather late for me) — Between the end of the Chatterley ban And the Beatles' first LP.*

Philip Larkin, *'Annus Mirabilis'* (1974) •924

*He who desires but acts not, breeds pestilence.*

William Blake, *The Marriage of Heaven and Hell* (1790-93) •925

*Had we but world enough, and time, This coyness, lady, were no crime.*

Andrew Marvell, *'To His coy Mistress'* (1681) •926

*Licence my roving hands,
and let them go,*

*Behind, before, above,
between, below.*

*O my America, my new
found land,*

*My kingdom, safeliest when
with one man manned.*

John Donne, *'To His Mistress
Going to Bed' (c.1595)* •927

*i like my body when it is with your
body. It is so quite a new thing.
Muscles better and nerves more.
i like your body. i like what it does,
i like its hows.*

e.e. cummings, *'Sonnets-Actualities'
no.8 (1925)* •928

# *But did they feel
the earth move?*

Ernest Hemingway, *For Whom the Bell Tolls
(1940)* •929

*Sex is more exciting on the
screen and between the pages
than between the sheets.*

Andy Warhol, *From A to B and
Back Again (1975)* •930

# *Reading about sex in
yesterday's novels is
liking watching people
smoke in old films.*

Novelist and scriptwriter Fay Weldon
in *the Guardian, 1 December 1989* •931

I've mostly written about sex by means of the space break.

Barbara Kingsolver, in *Writers on Writing: Collected Essays from the New York Times (2001)* •932

We have long past the Victorian era where asterisks were followed after a certain interval by a baby.

W. Somerset Maugham, *The Constant Wife (1926)* •933

Sex can be indicated with asterisks. I've always felt that was as good a way as any. John Dos Passos, in *George Plimpton (ed.) The Writer's Chapbook (1989)* •934

There is sex in the Discworld books, but it usually takes place two pages after the ending.

Terry Pratchett, in *Terry Pratchett and Stephen Briggs, The Discworld Companion (1994)* •935

Is it not strange that desire should so many years outlive performance?

William Shakespeare, *Henry IV, Part 2 (1597) II.iv* •936

¶

HANKY
PANKY

*Lolita, light of my life, fire of my loins My sin, my soul.*

Vladimir Nabokov, *Lolita (1955)* •940

*Give me chastity and continency — but not yet!*

St Augustine of Hippo, *Confessions (AD 397-8)* •937

*What is commonly called love, namely the desire of satisfying a voracious appetite with a certain quantity of delicate white human flesh.*

Henry Fielding, *Tom Jones (1749)* •941

# *What angel wakes me from my flowery bed?*

Titania to Bottom, despite his ass's head,
*A Midsummer Night's Dream III.i (1595)* •938

*He in a few minutes ravished this fair creature, or at least would have ravished her, if she had not, by a timely compliance, prevented him.*

Henry Fielding, *Jonathan Wild (1743)* •942

*He was as fressh as is the month of May.*

Chaucer, *The Canterbury Tales,*
*'The General Prologue'* •939

A little she strove, and
  much repented,
And whispering 'I will ne'er
  consent' — consented.

Lord Byron, *Don Juan (1819-24)* •943

A mistress should be
like a little country retreat
near the town, not to dwell
in constantly, but only
for a night and away.

William Wycherley,
*The Country Wife (1675)* •946

The reading or non-reading
a book — will never keep
down a single petticoat.

Lord Byron, *letter to Richard Hoppner,
29 October 1819* •944

Love is like linen; often
changed, the sweeter.

Phineas Fletcher, *Sicelides (performed 1614)* •947

Love ceases
to be pleasure
when it ceases
to be a secret.

English writer and adventuress
Aphra Behn •945

How happy I could
  be with either,
Were t'other dear
  charmer away!

John Gay, *The Beggar's Opera
(1728)* •948

*No visit to Dove Cottage, Grasmere, is complete without examining the outhouse where Hazlitt's father, a Unitarian minister of strong liberal views, attempted to put his hand up Dorothy Wordsworth's skirt.*

Alan Coren •949

# *A lover without indiscretion is no lover at all.*

Thomas Hardy, *The Hand of Ethelberta (1876)* •950

¶

# *TIME FOR REFLECTION*

*Food comes first, then morals.*

**Bertolt Brecht,** *Die Dreigroschenoper (1928)* ·951

Not to be born is,
past all prizing, best.

**Sophocles,** *Oedipus Coloneus* •952

Better is the end of a thing
than the beginning thereof.

Bible, *Eccliesiastes 7.8* •953

Never to have lived is best,  ancient writers say;

Never to have drawn the breath of life, never
to have looked into the eye of day;

The second best's a gay goodnight and
quickly turn away.

**W.B.Yeats,** 'From Oedipus at Colonus' (1928) •954

Birth, and copulation, and death.

That's all the facts when you come
to brass tacks:

Birth, copulation, and death.

I've been born, and once is enough.

**T.S. Eliot,** *Sweeney Agonistes (1932)* •955

Oh, isn't life
a terrible thing,
thank God?

**Dylan Thomas,** *Under Milk Wood (1954)* •956

Nothing happens,
nobody comes, nobody
goes, it's awful!

**Samuel Beckett,** *Waiting for Godot (1955)* •957

EXISTENCE

*This world is a comedy to those that think, a tragedy to those that feel.*

Horace Walpole, *letter to Anne, Countess of Upper Ossory, 16 August 1776* •958

*Laughter is pleasant, but the exertion is too much for me.*

Thomas Love Peacock, *Nightmare Abbey (1818)* •959

*Humour is emotional chaos remembered in tranquility.*

James Thurber, in *New York Post 29 February 1960* •960

*The funniest thing about comedy is that you never know why people laugh. I know what makes them laugh but trying to get your hands on the why of it is like trying to pick an eel out of a tub of water.*

W.C. Fields, in *R.J. Anobile, A Flask of Fields (1972)* •961

*Comedy is an imitation of the common errors of our life.*

Philip Sidney, *The Defence of Poetry (1595)* •962

*Well there you are. This is life. What I've found as a writer is that you have to keep taming it down, making it less improbable in order to fit it into some sort of fictional context.*

John Mortimer, in *Paris Review 1995* •963

*When Gregor Samsa awoke one morning from uneasy dreams he found himself transformed in his bed into a gigantic insect.*

Franz Kafka, *The Metamorphosis (1915)* •964

*A novel is balanced between a few true impressions and the multitude of false ones that make up the most of what we call life. It tells us that for every human being there is a diversity of existences, that the single existence is itself an illusion in part… it promises us meaning, harmony, and even justice.*

Saul Bellow, speech on receiving the Nobel Prize *1976* •965

*Imagination is not enough. Knowledge is necessary.*

Paul Scott, in *Hilary Spurling, Paul Scott (1990)* •966

*I distrust the incommunicable: it is the source of all violence.*

Jean-Paul Sartre, *'Qu'est-ce que la littérature?'* in *Les Temps Modernes July 1947* •967

*Woord is but wynd; leff woord and tak the dede.*

John Lydgate, *c.1370-c.1451, Secrets of Old Philosophers* •968

*Life, you know, is rather like opening a tin of sardines. We are all of us looking for the key. And, I wonder, how many of you here tonight have wasted years of your lives looking behind the kitchen dressers of this life for that key.*

Alan Bennett, *Beyond the Fringe, (1961 revue) 'Take a Pew'* •969

*It has long been an axiom of mine that the little things are infintely the most important.*

Arthur Conan Doyle, *Adventures of Sherlock Holmes (1892)* •970

*The only means of strengthening one's intellect is to make up one's mind about nothing — to let the mind be a thoroughfare for all my thoughts. Not a select party.*

John Keats, *letter to George and Georgiana Keats, 24 September 1819* •971

*The test of a first-rate intelligence is the ability to hold two opposed ideas in the mind at the same time, and still retain the ability to function.*

F. Scott Fitzgerald, *in Esquire February 1936, 'The Crack-Up'* •972

Pooh began to feel a little more comfortable, because when you are a Bear of Very Little Brain, and you Think of Things, you find sometimes that a Thing that seemed very Thingish inside you is quite different when it gets out in the open and has other people looking at it.

A.A. Milne, *The House at Pooh Corner (1928)* •973

If all the year were
  playing holidays,

To sport would be as
  tedious as to work;

But when they seldom come,
  they wished for come.

William Shakespeare,
*Henry IV, Part I (1597) I.ii* •976

# All intellectual improvement arises from leisure.

Samuel Johnson, in *Boswell, Life of Samuel Johnson (1791)* •974

# Life's not just being alive, but being well.

Martial, *AD c.40-c.104,Epigrammata* •977

What is this life if, full of care,
We have no time to stand and stare?

W.H. Davies, *'Leisure' (1911)* •975

*You should pray to have a sound mind in a sound body.*

Juvenal, *Satires* •978

*Noble deeds and hot baths are the best cures for depression.*

Dodie Smith, *I Capture the Castle (1949)* •979

*If a lot of cures are suggested for a disease, it means that the disease is incurable.*

Anton Chekhov, *The Cherry Orchard, Act.1 (1904)* •980

*I am but mad north-north-west; when the wind is southerly, I know a hawk from a handsaw.*

William Shakespeare, *Hamlet (1601) II.ii* •981

*I am never better than when I am mad. Then methinks I am a brave fellow; then I do wonders. But reason abuseth me, and there's the torment, there's the hell.*

Thomas Kyd, *The Spanish Tragedy (1592) The Fourth Addition* •982

*There is no greater sorrow than to recall a time of happiness.*

Dante •983

*For if the darkness and corruption
leave a vestige of the thoughts that
once I had, better by far you should
forget and smile than that you should
remember and be sad.*

Poet Christina Rossetti, *'Remember', 1862* •984

*Truth is the most
valuable thing
we have. Let us
economize it.*

Mark Twain, *Following the Equator (1897)* •987

*The past is a foreign county;
they do things differently there.*

L.P. Hartley, *The Go-Between (1953)* •985

*Time present and
time past
Are both perhaps
present in time future
And time future
contained in time past.*

T.S. Eliot, *Four Quartets
'Burnt Norton' (1936)* •986

*Tis strange — but true;
for truth is always strange;
stranger than fiction.*

Lord Byron, *Don Juan (1819-24)* •988

The truth is rarely pure, and never simple.

Oscar Wilde, *The Importance of Being Earnest (1895)* •989

What if this present were the world's last night?

John Donne, *Holy Sonnets (after 1609)* •990

All shall be well and all shall be well and all manner of things shall be well.

Julian of Norwich, 14th Century mystic, *Revelations of Divine Love* •991

*Vladimir: That passed the time.*

*Estragon: It would have passed anyway.*

*Vladimir: Yes, but not so rapidly.*

Samuel Beckett, *Waiting for Godot (1955)* •992

*Sir, more than kisses, let us mingle souls.*

John Donne, *'To Sir Henry Wotton' (1597-8)* •993

Know then thyself, presume
  not God to scan;

the proper study of mankind
  is man.

Alexander Pope, *An Essay on Man — Epistle 2
(1733)* •994

*Man is born to live,
not to prepare for life.*

Boris Pasternak, *Doctor Zhivago (1958)* •996

*People in life hardly
seem definite enough
to appear in print.*

Ivy Compton-Burnett, *attrib. in
Times Literary Supplement 29 May 1982* •995

Youth, what man's age is like to be doth show;
We may our ends by our beginnings know.

John Denham, *'Of Prudence' (1668)* •997

Men must be taught as if you
  taught them not,

And things unknown proposed
  as things forgot.

Alexander Pope, *An Essay
on Criticism (1711)* •998


# He can't think
# without his hat.

Samuel Beckett, *Waiting for Godot (1955)* •999


Men have had every advantage
of us in telling their own story.
Education has been theirs in so
much higher a degree; the pen
has been in their hands.

Jane Austen, *Persuasion (1818)* •1001


Western culture... was a grand
ancestral property that educated
men inherited from their intellectual
forefathers, while their female relatives,
like characters in a Jane Austen novel,
were relegated to modest dower houses
on the edge of the estate.

Sandra M. Gilbert, *'What Do
Feminist Critics Want?' (1980)* •1000


*A man who moralizes
is usually a hypocrite,
and a woman who moralizes
is invariably plain.*

Oscar Wilde, *Lady Windermere's Fan,
(1892)* •1002

*Conventionality is not morality. Self-righteousness is not religion. To attack the first is not to assail the last. To pluck the mask from the face of the Pharisee, is not to lift an impious hand to the Crown of Thorns.*

Charlotte Brontë, *Jane Eyre (2nd ed., 1848) preface* •1003

*It is particularly encumbent on those who never change their opinion to be secure of judging properly at first.*

Jane Austen, Lizzie Bennet in *Pride and Prejudice* •1004

*Vice is detestable; I banish all its appearances from my coteries; and I would banish its reality, too, were I sure I should then have any thing but empty chairs in my drawing-room.*

Fanny Burney, *Camilla (1796)* •1005

*Man is the Only Animal that Blushes. Or needs to.*

Mark Twain, *Following the Equator (1897)* •1006

*Man is the only animal that laughs and weeps; for he is the only animal that is struck by the difference between what things are, and what they ought to be.*

William Hazlitt, *Lectures on English Comic Writers (1818)* •1007

A tragic situation exists when virtue does not triumph but when it is still felt that man is nobler than the forces that destroy him.

**George Orwell,** *'Lear, Tolstoy and the Fool'* *(1947)* •1008

# Sport strips away personality, letting the white bone of character shine through.

**Rita Mae Brown,** *Sudden Death (1983)* •1009

What I know most surely about morality and the duty of man I owe to sport.

**Albert Camus, in** *Herbert R. Lottman,* *Albert Camus (1979)* •1010

# Man is a history-making creature who can neither repeat his past nor leave it behind.

**W.H. Auden,** *The Dyer's Hand (1962) 'D.H. Lawrence'* •1011

It is well to observe the force and virtue and consequence of discoveries, and these are to be seen nowhere more conspicuously than in those three which were unknown to the ancients, and of which the origins, though recent, are obscure and inglorious; namely, printing, gunpowder, and the mariner's needle [compass]. For these three have changed the whole face and state of things throughout the world.

**Francis Bacon,** *Novum Organum (1620)* •1012

*How quick come the reasons for approving what we like!*

Jane Austen, *Persuasion* •1013

*At some time in the future, if the human mind becomes something totally different from what it now is, we may learn to separate literary creation from intellectual honesty. At present we know only that the imagination, like certain wild animals, will not breed in captivity.*

George Orwell, *'The Prevention of Literature'* in *Polemic, January 1946* •1014

*We can't all be happy, we can't all be rich, we can't all be lucky… Some must cry so that others may be able to laugh the more heartily.*

Jean Rhys, *Good Morning, Midnight (1939)* •1015

*'Blessed is the man who expects nothing, for he shall never be disappointed' was the ninth beatitude.*

Alexander Pope, *letter to Fortescue, 23rd September 1725* •1016

*From envy are born hatred, detraction, calumny, joy caused by the misfortune of a neighbour, and displeasure caused by his prosperity.*

Gregory the Great (channeling Yoda?) •1017

*Here's the rule for bargains: 'Do other men, for they would do you.' That's the true business precept.*

Charles Dickens, *Martin Chuzzlewit (1844)* •1018

*We have just enough religion to make us hate, but not enough to make us love one another.*

Jonathan Swift, *Thoughts on Various Subjects (1711)* •1020

*If you pick up a starving dog and make him prosperous, he will not bite you. That is the principal difference between a dog and a man.*

Mark Twain •1019

*I sometimes think God, in creating man, somewhat overestimated his ability.* Oscar Wilde. •1021

Often it seems
a pity Noah
and his party
didn't miss
the boat.

Mark Twain •1022

Ah, but a man's reach
should exceed his grasp,
Or what's a heaven for?

Robert Browning, *'Andrea del Sarto' (1855)* •1023

¶

# Nature

The lark's on the wing;
The snail's on the thorn:
God's in his heaven —
All's right with the world!

Robert Browning, *Pippa Passes (1841)* •1024


And this our life, exempt
  from public haunt,
Finds tongues in trees,
  books in running brooks,
Sermons in stones, and
  good in everything.

William Shakespeare,
*As You Like It (1599)* •1025


There is a place in
  the pathless woods,
There is a rapture on
  the lonely shore,
There is a society, where
  none intrudes,
By the deep sea,
  and music in its roar:
I love not man the less,
  but nature more.

Lord Byron, *Childe Harold's Pilgrimage
(1812-18)* •1026


After you have exhausted what
there is in business, politics,
conviviality, and so on — have
found that none of these finally
satisfy, or permanently wear —
what remains? Nature remains.

Walt Whitman, *Specimen Days and Collect
(1882)* •1027

*Give me odorous at sunrise a garden of beautiful flowers where I can walk undisturbed.*

Walt Whitman, *Give Me the Splendid Silent Sun* (**pub. in** *Leaves of Grass, 1900*) •1028

*People from a planet without flowers would think we must be mad with joy the whole time to have such things about us.*

Iris Murdoch, *A Fairly Honourable Defeat (1970)* •1029

*Summer afternoon — summer afternoon… the two most beautiful words in the English language.*

Henry James; in *Edith Wharton, A Backward Glance (1934)* •1030

*Just living is not enough… One must have sunshine, freedom, and a little flower.*

Hans Christian Andersen •1031

*The most beautiful things in the world are the most useless — peacocks and lilies for instance.*

John Ruskin •1032

*While the earth remaineth, seedtime and harvest, and cold and heat, and summer and winter, and day and night shall not cease.*

Bible, Genesis 8:22 •1033

*'I play for Seasons; not Eternities!'*
*Says Nature.*

George Meredith, *Modern Love (1862)* •1034

*Gie me ae spark o' Nature's fire,*
*That's a' the learning I desire.*

Robert Burns, *'First Epistle to Lapraik' (1785)* •1035

# All good things are artificial, for nature is the art of God.

Sir Thomas Browne, *Religio Medici (1643)* •1036

*She had never seen a place of which nature had done more, or where natural beauty had been so little counteracted by an awkward taste.*

Jane Austen, *Pride & Prejudice.* Elizabeth's first view of Pemberley, believed to be based on Chatsworth House. •1037

*Nothing is more the child of art than a garden.*

Sir Walter Scott •1038

*Man masters nature not by force but by understanding.*

English poet and dramatist Robert Bridges, *attr.* •1039

Trees sing and dance, make faces and give flower bouquets, trying to be loved. You ever notice that trees do everything to get attention we do, except walk? Alice Walker, *The Color Purple* •1040

No matter how often you knock at nature's door, she won't answer in words you can understand — for Nature is dumb. She'll vibrate and moan like a violin, but you mustn't expect a song.

Ivan Turgenev, *On the Eve (1860)* •1041

'We can talk,' said the Tiger-lily, 'when there's anybody worth talking to.'

Lewis Carroll, *Through the Looking-Glass (1872)* •1042

But when Beryl looked at the bush, it seemed to her the bush was sad. We are dumb trees, reaching up in the night, imploring we know not what, said the sorrowful bush.

Katherine Mansfield, *'The Garden Party' (1922)* •1043

I have learned
To look on nature, not as in the hour
Of thoughtless youth; but hearing often-times
The still, sad music of humanity.

William Wordsworth, *'Lines composed a few miles above Tintern Abbey' (1798)* •1044

Nature is unforgiving; she will not agree to withdraw her flowers, her music, her scents or her rays of light before the abominations of man.

Victor Hugo, *Ninety-three (1874)* •1045

*The best remedy for those who are afraid, lonely or unhappy is to go outside, somewhere where they can be quiet, alone with the heavens, nature and God. Because only then does one feel that all is as it should be...*

Anne Frank, *The Diary of Anne Frank* *(1947)* •1046

¶

# MONEY MAKES THE WORLD GO ROUND

*Writing is one-tenth perspiration and nine-tenths masturbation.*

**Alan Bennett** ·1047

*Only amateurs say they write for their own amusement. Writing is not an amusing occupation. It is a combination of ditch-digging, mountain-climbing, treadmill and childbirth. Writing may be interesting, absorbing, exhilarating, racking, relieving. But amusing? Never!*

Edna Ferber, *A Peculiar Treasure (1939)* •1050

*89% work and worry over work, struggle against lunacy 10%, and friends 1%.*

Tennessee Williams with a breakdown of his life; *John Lahr, Light Fantastic (1996)* •1048

*How one likes to suffer. Anyway writers do; it is their income.*

W.H. Auden, *Berlin diary, April 1929* •1051

*Writing is not a profession but a vocation of unhappiness.*

Georges Simenon; *interview in Paris Review Summer 1955* •1049

*I am a galley slave to pen and ink.*

Honoré de Balzac, *letter 1832* •1052

It was labour-intensive work, scriptorium-slow.

Seamus Heaney on translating *Beowulf*; *Beowulf (1999) Introduction* ·1053

It bored me hellishly to write the Emigrant; well, it's going to bore others to read it; that's only fair.

Robert Louis Stevenson, *letter to Sidney Colvin, January 1880* ·1054

Three hours a day will produce as much as a man ought to write.

Anthony Trollope, *Thackeray (1879)* ·1055

You know, it's not exactly a natural pursuit, a man putting himself in front of a typewriter — a machine — day after day. But you've got to spend three or four years digging yourself a rut so deep that finally you find it more convenient not to get out of it. Ernest Haycox, in *Ernest Haycox (1996)* ·1056

Only habit of persistent work can make one continually content; it produces an opium that numbs the soul.

Gustave Flaubert, *Letter 26 July 1851* ·1057

*Nature is monstrously unjust. There is no substitute for talent. Industry and all the virtues are of no avail.*

Aldous Huxley, in *George Greenfield, Scribblers for Bread (1989)* •1058

*The solitary genius in the garret is a male myth, as he would undoubtedly have been supported by several unacknowledged women who cooked and ironed.*

Michèle Roberts, in *Independent on Sunday 4 February 1996* •1059

*Literature cannot be the business of a woman's life, because of the sacredness of her duties at home.*

Robert Southey on Charlotte Brontë •1060

*Only ambitious nonentities and hearty mediocrities exhibit their rough drafts. It's like passing around samples of one's sputum.*

Vladimir Nabokov •1061

*The pleasure of the first draft lies in deceiving yourself that it is quite close to the real thing. The pleasure of the subsequent drafts lies partly in realizing that you haven't been gulled by the first draft.*

Julian Barnes, in *Paris Review Winter 2000* •1062

*It's nice to have company when you come face to face with a blank page.*

George S. Kaufman on collaboration, in *Howard Teichman, George S. Kaufman: an Intimate Portrait (1973)* •1063

*No man but a blockhead ever wrote, except for money.*

Samuel Johnson, in *Boswell, Life of Samuel Johnson (1791) 5 April 1776* •1064

*Were I my own man... I would refuse this offer (with all gratitude); but as I am situated, L.300 or L.400 a-year is not to be sneezed at.*

Sir Walter Scott sees the value of the Laureateship; *letter to James Ballantyne, 24 August 1813* •1066

*The profession of letters is, after all, the only one in which one can make no money without being ridiculous.*

Jules Renard, *Diary 1906* •1065

*I'm a jobbing writer, like everyone else.*

Fay Weldon on why she agreed to write a product-placement novel commissioned by a jewellery company. •1067

*Some day I hope to write a book where the royalties will pay for the copies I give away.*

Clarence Darrow, American lawyer •1068

*Crime does not pay — enough.*

Clayton Rawson, founder of Mystery Writers of America; in *American Heritage Dictionary of American Quotations (1997)* •1069

*My object is renumeration.*

Frances Hodgson Burnett, submitting her first short story for magazine publication; *letter c.1867* •1070

*For me I never cared for fame Solvency was my only aim.*

British poet and editor J.C. Squire, at a dinner given in his honour, *15 December 1932* •1071

*Many books are written…for very mundane reasons. It tends to be forgotten, for example, that Johnson wrote Rasselas to defray the expenses of his mother's funeral, or that Dumas's terse, interrogative dialogue was the result of his being paid at so many centimes a line.*

D.J. Taylor, *After the War (1993)* •1072

*Write without pay until somebody offers you pay. If nobody offers within three years the candidate may look upon the circumstance with the most implicit confidence as the sign that sawing wood is what he was intended for.*

Mark Twain •1073

*Just try doing your VAT return with a head full of goblins.*

Terry Pratchett on whether he lives in his fantasy world. •1074

*I have just received nearly twenty pounds myself on the second edition of 'Sense and Sensibility' which gives me a fine flow of literary ardour.*

Jane Austen •1075

*It's about to make me rich.*

Tom Stoppard, in response to the question 'what is *Rosencrantz and Guildenstern are Dead* about?' after its first night in New York; in *Independent* 2 December 1995 •1076

¶

*All you need in life is ignorance and confidence; then success is sure.*

**Mark Twain,** *letter to Mrs Foote, 2 December 1887* •1077

*Modern fame is too often a crown of thorns, and brings all the vulgarity of the world upon you. I sometimes wish I had never written a line.*

**Alfred, Lord Tennyson,** in conversation with Marie Corelli; *Theresa Ransom, The Mysterious Miss Marie Corelli (1999)* •1079

*It took me fifteen years to discover I had no talent for writing, but I couldn't give it up because by that time I was too famous.*

**Robert Benchley,** quoted in *Robert Benchley, by Nat Benchley, 1955,* •1078

*Celebrity is a mask that eats into the face.*

**John Updike,** *Self-Consciousness: Memoirs (1989)* •1080

For a writer, success is always temporary, success is only a delayed failure. And it is incomplete.

Graham Greene, *A Sort of Life (1931)* •1083

The best fame is a writer's fame: it's enough to get a table at a good restaurant, but not enough that you get interrupted when you eat.

Fran Lebowitz, in *Observer 30 May 1993, 'Sayings of the Week'* •1081

The common idea that success spoils people by making them vain, egotistic, and self-complacent is erroneous; on the contrary it makes them, for the most part, humble, tolerant, and kind. Failure makes people bitter and cruel.

W. Somerset Maugham, *The Summing Up (1938)* •1084

The usual drawback to success is that it annoys one's friends so.

P.G. Wodehouse, *'The Man Upstairs', (1914)* •1082

Fools admire everything in a respected author.

Voltaire, *Candide (1759)* •1085

*Even for learned men, love of fame is the last thing to be given up.*

Tacitus, *Histories* •1086

*I should so much have loved to be popular!*

Henry James, in *Alfred Sutro Celebrities and Simple Souls (1933)*•1087

*A best-seller was a book which somehow sold well simply because it was selling well.*

US librarian, historian, lawyer and writer Daniel Boorstin, *The Image (1962)* •1088

*A best-seller is the gilded tomb of a mediocre talent.*

Logan Pearsall Smith, *Afterthoughts (1931)* •1089

*My Rome praises my little books, loves them, recites them; I am in every pocket, every hand.* Martial, *Epigrammata* •1090

When one says that a writer is fashionable one practically always means that he is admired by people under thirty.

George Orwell ·1091

In America only the successful writer is important, in France all writers are important, in England no writer is important, in Australia you have to explain what a writer is.

Geoffrey Cotterell, *New York Journal, 1961* ·1093

'The Ancient Mariner' would not have taken so well if it had been called 'The Old Sailor'.

Samuel Butler *(1835-1902), attrib.* ·1092

*Ever tried. Ever failed. No matter. Try again. Fail again. Fail better.*

Samuel Beckett, *Worstward Ho (1983)* ·1094

# Publish And Be Damned

## No author is a man of genius to his publisher.

Heinrich Heine, German Poet. •1095

*An editor is one who separates the wheat from the chaff and prints the chaff.*

Adlai Stevenson, *The Stevenson Wit (1966)* •1097

*I object to publishers: the one service they have done me is to teach me to do without them. They combine commercial rascality with artistic touchiness and pettiness, without being either good business men or fine judges of literature.*

George Bernard Shaw •1096

*Everywhere I go I'm asked if I think the universities stifle writers. My opinion is that they don't stifle enough of them. There's many a best-seller that could have been prevented by a good teacher.*

Flannery O'Connor, in
*The Writer's Craft (1974)* •1098

*All a publisher has to do is write cheques at intervals, while a lot of deserving and industrious chappies rally round and do the real work.*

P.G. Wodehouse, *My Man Jeeves (1919)* •1099

*Our Grubstreet biographers watch for the death of a great man, like so many undertakers, on purpose to make a penny out of him.*

Joseph Addison, *Freeholder (1715-16)* •1102

*There is only one way to make money at writing, and that is to marry a publisher's daughter.*

George Orwell, *Down and Out in Paris and London (1933)* •1100

*Publishing is not ordinary trade: it is gambling. The publisher bets the cost of manufacturing, advertising and circulating a book, plus the overhead of his establishment, against every book he publishes exactly as a turf bookmaker bets against every horse in the race.*

George Bernard Shaw, in *The Author, Summer 1945* •1101

*There's never been much love lost between literature and the market. The consumer economy loves a product that sells at a premium, wears out quickly or is susceptible to regular improvement… A classic work of literature is inexpensive, infinitely re-usable, and, worst of all, unimprovable.* Jonathan Franzen, *How to be Alone? (2002) 'Why bother?'* •1103

Though our publishers will tell you that they are ever seeking 'original writers', nothing could be farther from the truth. What they want is more of the same, only thinly disguised...What the public wants, no one knows. Not even the publishers.

Henry Miller, 'When I Reach for My Revolver' (1955) •1104

The shelf-life of the modern hardback writer is somewhere between the milk and the yoghurt.

Calvin Trillin, in Sunday Times 9 June 1991; attrib. •1105

Good editors are really the third eye. Cool. Dispassionate. They don't love you or your work; for me that is what is valuable — not compliments. Sometimes it's uncanny; the editor puts his or her finger on exactly the place the writer knows is weak...

Toni Morrison, in Women Writers at Work: The Paris Review Interviews (1998) •1106

[The editor] should say to himself, 'How can I help this writer to say it better in his own style?' and avoid 'How can I show him how I would write it, if it were my piece?'

James Thurber in a memo to New Yorker in 1959, reprinted in New York Times Book Review 4 December 1988 •1107

You cannot or at least should not try to argue with authors. Too many are like children whose tears can suddenly be changed to smiles if they are handled in the right way.

A publisher's view from Michael Joseph, The Adventure of Publishing (1949) •1108

*I've had great fun doing some stories by phone with certain magazine editors... Bargaining goes on, horse-trading. 'You can have the dash if I can get the semicolon.'*

Margaret Atwood, in an interview, March 1986; in Paris Review Winter 1990 •1109

*The author's agent fosters in authors the greed for an immediate money return... at the cost of all dignity and repose.*

William Heinemann, in The Author, c.1890 — in George Greenfield, Scribblers for Bread (1989) •1112

# No need to change the title. Easier to change publishers.

Graham Greene, in a telegram to his American publishers after they responded to the manuscript of his Travels with my Aunt with 'Terrific book, but we'll need to change the title': •1110

*Talking of agents, when I opened the morning paper one morning last week I saw that it had finally happened: somebody shot one. It was probably for the wrong reasons but at least it was a step in the right direction.*

Raymond Chandler, letter to Charles Morton 17 December 1951 •1113

*Never buy an editor or publisher a lunch or a drink until he has brought an article story or book from you. This rule is absolute and may be broken only at your peril.*

John Creasey, British crime writer. •1111

*A good many young writers make the mistake of enclosing a stamped, self-addressed envelope, big enough for the manuscript to come back in. This is too much of a temptation to the editor.* Ring Lardner, How to Write Short Stories (1924) preface •1114

My story 'The Sea and Its Shore' came back from The Criterion with two rejection slips enclosed, which seems unnecessarily cruel.

Elizabeth Bishop, *letter to Marianne Moore, 25 February 1937* •1115

I will carry on writing, to be sure. But I don't know if I would want to publish again.

J.K. Rowling, author of the *Harry Potter* Books. •1118

The book of my enemy
   has been remaindered
And I am pleased.

Brian James, Australian writer; *The Book of My Enemy Has Been Remaindered* •1116

Publish and be damned.

Duke Of Wellington's reply to a threat of blackmail from Harriette Wilson, *c.1825; attrib* •1119

I have an exceedingly odd sensation, when I consider that... a work which was so lately lodged in all privacy, in my bureau may now be seen by every butcher and baker, cobbler and tinker, throughout the three kingdoms, for the small tribute of three pence.

Fanny Burney on the perils of publication; *Diary, March 1778* •1117

¶

*A merchant shall hardly keep himself from doing wrong.*

Bible, Ecclesiastes 26.29 •1122

*If possible honestly, if not somehow, make money.*

**Horace,** *Epistles* •1120

*Money, which represents the prose of life, and which is hardly spoken of in parlours without an apology, is, in its effects and laws, as beautiful as roses.*

**Ralph Waldo Emerson,** *Essays, Second Series (1844) 'Nominalist and Realist'* •1123

*Get place and wealth, if possible, with grace;*
*If not, by any means get wealth and place.*

**Alexander Pope,** *Imitations of Horace (1738)* •1121

*A large income is the best recipe for happiness I ever heard of.*

Jane Austen, Mary Crawford in *Mansfield Park (1814)* •1124

*We are all Adam's children but silk makes the difference.*

Thomas Fuller, *Gnomologia (1732)* •1125

*A single woman, with a very narrow income, must be a ridiculous disagreeable old maid! the proper sport of boys and girls; but a single woman of good fortune, is always respectable, and may be sensible and pleasant as anybody else.*

Jane Austen, Emma in *Emma (1815)* •1126

*Business, you know, may bring money, but friendship hardly ever does.*

Jane Austen, Mr Knightley in *Emma (1815)*•1127

*It is very difficult for the prosperous to be humble.*

Jane Austen, Frank Churchill in *Emma (1815)* •1128

*Plenty has made me poor.*

Ovid, *Metamorphoses* •1129

*But there are certainly not so many men of large fortune in the world as there are pretty women to deserve them.*

Jane Austen, *Mansfield Park (1814)* •1130

*Money can only give happiness where there is nothing else to give.*

Jane Austen, Marianne in
*Sense and Sensibility (1811)* •1131

*We all need money, but there are degrees of desperation.*

Anthony Burgess, in *Face, December 1984* •1132

*All decent people live beyond their incomes nowadays, and those who aren't respectable live beyond other peoples'.*

Saki, *Chronicles of Clovis (1911)* •1133

*Annual income twenty pounds, annual expenditure nineteen nineteen six, result happiness. Annual income twenty pounds, annual expenditure twenty pounds ought and six, result misery.*

Charles Dickens,
*David Copperfield (1850)* •1134

*I can get no remedy against this consumption of the purse: borrowing only lingers and lingers it out, but the disease is incurable.* William Shakespeare,
*Henry IV, Part 2 (1597) I.ii*
•1135

*Dreading that climax of all human ills, The inflammation of his weekly bills.*

Lord Byron, *Don Juan (1819-24)* •1136

*Economy is going without something you do want in case you should, some day, want something you probably won't want.*

Anthony Hope, *The Dolly Dialogues (1894)* •1137

*I'm tired of Love: I'm still more
  tired of Rhyme.*

*But Money gives me pleasure
  all the time.*

Hillaire Belloc, *'Fatigued' (1923)* •1138

¶

# AFFAIRS OF STATE

For forms of government let fools contest;
Whate'er is best administered is best.

**Alexander Pope**, *An Essay on Man,
Epistle 3* ·1139

# Government

I would not give half a guinea to live under one form of government than another. It is of no moment to the happiness of an individual.

Samuel Johnson, in Boswell, Life of Samuel Johnson (1791), 31 March 1772 •1140

An election is coming. Universal peace is declared, and the foxes have a sincere interest in prolonging the lives of the poultry.

George Eliot, Felix Holt (1866) •1141

In mobilizing support for a project or policy it is especially agreeable to be able to call upon the distinguished dead; their distinction adds intellectual weight and moral force to the argument, and their death makes it impossible for them to appear on television later and say that they meant something completely different.

Antony Jay, introduction to Oxford Dictionary of Political Quotations (1996) •1142

No writer before the middle of the 19th century wrote about the working classes other than as grotesque or as pastoral decoration. Then when they were given the vote certain writers started to suck up to them.

Evelyn Waugh, in Paris Review 1963 •1143

*Political language… is designed to make lies sound truthful and murder respectable, and to give an appearance of solidity to pure wind.* George Orwell, *Shooting an Elephant (1950) 'Politics and the English Language'* •1144

*Good people do not need laws to tell them to act responsibly, while bad people will find a way around the laws.*

Plato •1146

*My faith in the people governing is, on the whole, infinitesimal; my faith in The People governed is, on the whole, illimitable.*

Charles Dickens, speech at Birmingham and Midland Institute, *27 September 1869* •1145

*Good laws, if they are not obeyed, do not constitute good government.*

Aristotle •1147

# More laws, less justice.

Cicero •1148

The more corrupt the state,
the more numerous the laws.

Tacitus •1149

If the law supposes that,'
said Mr Bumble... 'the
law is a ass — a idiot.'

Charles Dickens, *Oliver Twist (1838)* •1152

# The rusty curb of old father antick, the law.

William Shakespeare, *Henry IV, Part I
(1597) I.ii* •1150

People must not do things for
fun. We are not here for fun.
There is no reference to fun
in any Act of Parliament.

A.P. Herbert, *Uncommon Law (1935)* •1151

# The one great principle of the English law is, to make business for itself.

Charles Dickens,
*Bleak House (1853)* •1153

*The law is reason free from passion.*
Aristotle •1154

*It seems to me the mark of a civilised society is that certain privileges should be taken for granted such as education, health care and the safety to walk the streets.*
Alan Bennett •1155

*Because it is difficult to join them together, it is much safer for a prince to be feared  than loved, if he is to fail in one of the two.*
Niccolò Machiavelli, *The Prince (written 1513)* •1156

*Men of power have no time to read; yet the men who do not read are unfit for power.*
Michael Foot •1157

*Dictators are as scared of books as they are of cannon.*
Harry Golden, *Only in America (1958)* •1158

*BATTLE,* n., *A method of untying with the teeth a political knot that would not yield to the tongue.*

Ambrose Bierce, *The Cynic's Word Book (1906)* •1161

*Laws are silent in time of war.*

Cicero, *Pro Milone* •1159

*War is capitalism with the gloves off and many who go to war know it but they go to war because they don't want to be a hero.*

Tom Stoppard, *Travesties (1975)* •1162

# Force, and fraud, are in war the two cardinal virtues.

Thomas Hobbes, *Leviathan (1651)* •1160

*Dulce et decorum est pro patria mori. — It is sweet and fitting to die for one's country.*

Horace, *Odes* •1165

*How is the world ruled and led to war? Diplomats lie to journalists and believe these lies when they seem them in print.*

Karl Kraus, *Nachts (1918)* •1163

*If you could hear, at every jolt, the blood*
*Come gargling from the froth-corrupted lungs,*
*Obscene as cancer, bitter as the cud*
*Of vile, incurable sores on innocent tongues, —*
*My friend, you would not tell with such high zest*
*To children ardent for some desperate glory,*
*The old Lie: Dulce et decorum est Pro patria mori.*

Wilfred Owen, *'Dulce et Decorum Est' (1918)* •1166

*'My country, right or wrong' is a thing no patriot would think of saying except in a desperate case. It is like saying, 'My mother drunk or sober'.*

G.K. Chesterton, *Defendant, 1901.* •1164

# An author's first duty is to let down his country.

Brendan Behan,
*The Guardian, 1960* •1167

*I am a soldier, convinced that I am acting on behalf of soldiers. I believe that this war, upon which I entered as a war of defence and liberation, has now become a war of aggression and conquest. I believe that the purposes for which I and my fellow-soldiers entered upon this war should have been clearly stated as to have made it impossible to change them, and that, had this been done, the objects which actuated us would now be attainable by negotiation.*

Siegfried Sassoon, *'A Soldier's Declaration'* addressed to his commanding officer and sent to the *Bradford Pioneer July 1917* •1169

*Who live under the shadow of a war,*
*What can I do that matters?*

Stephen Spender, *'Who live under the shadow of a war' (1933)* •1168

*What passing-bells for those*
  *who die as cattle?*
*Only the monstrous anger of*
  *the guns.*
*Only the stuttering rifles'*
  *rapid rattle*
*Can patter out their*
  *hasty orisons.*

Poet Wilfred Owen, *'Anthem for Doomed Youth', 1917.* •1170

*God is on the side not of the heavy battalions, but of the best shots.*

Voltaire, 'The Piccini Notebooks' (c.1735-50) •1171

*Was none who would be foremost
To lead such dire attack;
But those behind cried 'Forward!'
And those before cried 'Back!'*

Lord Macaulay, 'Horatius' (1842) •1172

*Once more unto the breach,
    dear friends, once more;
Or close up the wall with our
    English dead!
In peace there's nothing so
    becomes a man
As modest stillness and humility:
But when the blast of war blows
    in our ears,
Then imitate the action of the tiger;
Stiffen the sinews, summon
    up the bloody,
Disguise fair nature with
    hard-favoured rage;
Then lend the eye a terrible aspect.*

William Shakespeare,
Henry V (1599) III.i •1173

*He saith among the trumpets, Ha ha; and he
smelleth the battle afar off, the thunder of the
captains, and the shouting.* Bible, Job 39:25 •1174

*See, the conquering hero comes!
Sound the trumpets, beat the drums!*

English librettist Thomas Morell,
Judas Maccabeus (1747) •1175

Every man thinks meanly of himself for not having been a soldier, or not having been at sea.

Samuel Johnson, in *Boswell's Life of Johnson (1791), 10 April 1778* •1176

You can always tell an old soldier by the inside of his holsters and cartridge boxes. The young ones carry pistols and cartridges; the old ones, grub. George Bernard Shaw, *Arms and the Man (1898)* •1177

As a general rule television is better than words in newspapers at communicating wars, and words are better than television at communicating peace.

Nicholas Tomalin, in *Listener 29 April 1971* •1178

So you're the little woman who wrote the book that made this great war!

Abraham Lincoln on meeting Harriet Beecher Stowe; *attrib.* •1179

The real war will never get in the books. And so goodbye to the war.

Walt Whitman, writing after the Ameican Civil War; *Specimen Days (1882) 'The Real War Will Never Get in the Books'* •1180

We make war that we may live in peace.

Aristotle, *Nicomachean Ethics* •1181

War always finds a way.

Bertolt Brecht, *Mother Courage (1939)* •1182

¶

*Beneath the rule of men entirely great*
*The pen is mightier than the sword.*

George Bulwer-Lytton, *Richelieu (1839)* •1183

*Books cannot be killed by*
*fire. People die, but books*
*never die. No man and no*
*force can abolish memory…*
*In this war, we know, books*
*are weapons. And it is a*
*part of your dedication*
*always to make them*
*weapons for man's freedom.*

Franklin D. Roosevelt, *'Message to the*
*Booksellers of America' 6 May 1942* •1184

*A good newspaper,*
*I suppose, is a nation*
*talking to itself.*

Arthur Miller, in *Observer*
*26 November 1961* •1185

*All a poet can do today is warn.*

Wilfred Owen; *preface (written 1918)* in
*Poems (1963)* •1186

Nothing I wrote in
the thirties saved one
Jew from Auschwitz.

W.H. Auden, *attrib.* •1187

Whenever books will be burned,
men also, in the end, are burned.

Heinrich Heine, *Almansor (1823)* •1188

I disapprove of what
you say, but I will
defend to the death
your right to say it.

Voltaire's attitude towards Helvetius following
the burning of the latter's *De l'esprit* in 1759.
Attributed to Voltaire, the words are in fact
S.G. Tallentyre's summary in *The Friends of
Voltaire (1907)* •1189

Freedom of the press
is guaranteed only to
those who own one.

A.J. Liebling, *'The Wayward Press:
Do you belong in Journalism?' (1960)* •1190

A censor is a man who
knows more than he
thinks you ought to.

Laurence J. Peter, Canadian educator known
for his 'Peter Principle', *attrib. 1982* •1191

I dislike censorship. Like an appendix
it is useless when inert and dangerous
when active. Politician and novelist
Maurice Edelman,
*attrib. 1982* •1192

*It takes away any desire you have to express yourself freely; whenever you write, you get a feeling there's a bone stuck in your throat.*

Anton Chekhov on Russian censorship, letter 19 January 1895 •1193

*I suppose that writers should, in a way, feel flattered by the censorship laws. They show a primitive fear and dread at the fearful magic of print.*

John Mortimer, Clinging to the Wreckage (1982) •1194

*It would be absurd to think that a book can cause riots.*

Salman Rushdie, to Indian interviewer in September 1988; his book The Satanic Verses invoked a fatwah against him. In Sunday Times 23 July 1989 •1195

*To be arrested for the power of your writing is one of the highest compliments an author can be paid, if an unwelcome one.*

Kenyan author Ngugi wa Thiong'o on being imprisoned without trial, in 1977; attrib. •1196

*What is a rebel? A man who says no.*

Albert Camus, L'Homme révolté (1951) •1197

The men who ordained and supervised this show of shame, this tragic charade, are frightened by the word, the power of ideas, the power of the pen… They are so scared of the word that they do not read. And that will be their funeral.

Nigerian writer and activist Ken Saro-Wiwa, shortly before his execution in 1995; in *London Review of Books 4 April 1996* •1198

The bravest are surely those who have the clearest vision of what is before them, glory and danger alike, and yet notwithstanding, go out to meet it.

Thucydides •1199

Lord take my soul, but the struggle continues.

Last words of Ken Saro-Wiwa before he was hanged; in *Daily Telegraph 13 November 1995* •1200

¶

# DEATH

Dying,
Is an art, like everything else.

**Plath,** *'Lady Lazarus' (1963)* •1201

*Death and taxes and childbirth! There's never a convenient time for any of them.* Margaret Mitchell, *Gone With the Wind (1936)* •1202

*Golden lads and girls all must, As chimney-sweepers, come to dust.*

William Shakespeare, *Cymbeline (1610) IV.ii* •1203

*Just try and set death aside. It sets you aside, and that's the end of it.* Ivan Turgenev, *Fathers and Sons (1862)* •1205

*The ceaseless labour of your life is to build the house of death.*

Montaigne, *Essais (1580)* •1204

*Death must be disntinguished from dying, with which it is often confused.*

Sydney Smith, in *H. Pearson, The Smith of the Smiths (1934)* •1206

*I know death hath ten thousand several doors for men to take their exits.*

Dramatist John Webster, *The Duchess of Malfi, (1623) IV.ii* •1207

Life is a great surprise. I do not see why death shouldn't be an even greater one. Vladimir Nabokov, *Pale Fire (1962)* •1208

It's not that I'm afraid to die. I just don't want to be there when it happens. Woody Allen, *Death (1975)* •1212

To die will be an awfully big adventure. J.M. Barrie, *Peter Pan (1928)* •1209

*If this is dying, I don't think much of it.* Lytton Strachey, last words, in *Michael Holroyd, Lytton Strachey, vol.2 (1968)* •1213

It matters not how a man dies, but how he lives. The act of dying is not of importance, it lasts so short a time. Critic and lexicographer Samuel Johnson, cited in *James Boswell, Life of Samuel Johnson, 1791* •1210

Nothing really wrong with him — only anno domini, but that's the most fatal complaint of all, in the end. James Hilton, *Goodbye, Mr Chips (1934)* •1214

Well, I've had a happy life. William Hazlitt 1778-1830, last words, In *W.C. Hazlitt, Memoirs of William Hazlitt (1867)* •1211

*God damn you all: I told you so.*

H.G. Wells suggests his own epitaph, in
conversation with Ernest Barker, 1939
— in *Ernest Barker, Age and Youth (1953)* •1215

*I am about to take
my last voyage, a
great leap in the dark.*

Thomas Hobbes, 1588-1679, in *John Watkins,
Anecdotes of Men of Learning (1808)* •1216

*To die: to sleep;*

*No more; and, by a sleep to say we end*

*The heart-ache and the thousand
  natural shocks*

*That flesh is heir to, 'tis a consummation*

*Devoutly to be wished. To die, to sleep;*

*To sleep: perchance to dream: ay,
  there's the rub;*

*For in that sleep of death what
  dreams may come*

*When we have shuffled off
  this mortal coil,*

*Must give us pause.*

William Shakespeare, *Hamlet (1601) III.i* •1217

*Men talk of killing
time, while time
quietly kills them.*

Dion Boucicault, *London Assurance (1841)* •1218

*Time goes, you say? Ah no!
Alas, Time stays, we go.*

Henry Austin Dobson, *'The Paradox of Time'
(1877)* •1219

*I had an interest in death from
an early age. It fascinated me.
When I heard 'Humpty Dumpty
sat on a wall,' I thought, 'Did
he fall or was he pushed?'*

P.D. James, in *Paris Review 1995* •1220

*Murder itself is not interesting. It is the impetus to murder, the passions and terrors which bring it to pass and the varieties of feelings surrounding the act that make a sordid or revolting event compulsive fascination. Even the most ardent readers of detective fiction are not much preoccupied with whether a Colt Magnum revolver or a Bowie knife was used to dispatch the victim. The perpetrator's purpose, the 'why', is what impels them to read on.*

Ruth Rendell, introduction to *The Reason Why: An Anthology of the Murderous Mind (1995)* •1221

*If the desire to kill and the opportunity to kill came always together, who would escape hanging?*

Mark Twain •1222

*Murder is always a mistake… One should never do anything that one cannot talk about after dinner.*

Oscar Wilde, *The Picture of Dorian Gray, 1891* •1223

The thought of suicide is a great consolation: by means of it one gets successfully through many a bad night.

Friedrich Wilhelm Nietzsche, *Beyond Good and Evil, 1896.* •1224

When one man dies, one chapter is not torn out of the book, but translated into a better language.

John Donne, *Devotions upon Emergent Occassions (1624)* •1227

Any man's death diminishes me, because I am involved in Mankind; And therefore never send to know for whom the bell tolls; it tolls for thee.

John Donne, *Devotions upon Emergent Occassions (1624)* •1225

Non omnis moriar. — I shall not altogether die.

Horace, *Odes* •1226

The dead don't die. They look on and help.

D.H. Lawrence, *letter to John Middleton Murry, 2 February 1923* •1228

*Finish, good lady;*
*the bright day is done,*
*And we are for the dark.*

William Shakespeare, *Anthony and Cleopatra (1606-7) V.ii* •1231

*The life of the dead consists in being present in the minds of the living.*

Cicero •1229

*Sunt lacrimae rerum et mentem mortalia tangunt. — There are tears shed for things even here and mortality touches the heart.*

Virgil, *Aeneid* •1232

*All writers learn from the dead. As long as you continue to write, you continue to explore the work of writers who have preceded you; you also feel judged and held to account by them.*

Margaret Atwood, *Negotiating with the Dead: A Writer on Writing (2002)* •1230

*Everywhere she dies. Everywhere I go she dies.*

*No sunrise, no city square, no lurking beautiful mountain but has her death in it.*

*The silence of her dying sounds through the carousel of language, it's a web on which laughter stitches itself. How can my hand clasp another's when between them is that thick death, that intolerable distance.*

Scottish poet Norman MacGaig, *'Memorial', in The White Bird (1973)* •1233

He first deceased;
  she for a little tried
To live without him:
  liked it not, and died.

Henry Wotton, *'Upon the Death of
Sir Albertus Moreton's Wife' (1651)* •1234

For all the happiness
  mankind can gain,
Is not in pleasure, but
  in rest from pain.

John Dryden, *The Indian Emperor (1665)* •1237

But there, everything has its
drawbacks, as the man said
when his mother-in-law died,
and they came down upon
him for the funeral expenses.

Jerome K. Jerome, *Three Men in a Boat (1889)* •1235

What I like about Clive
Is that he is no longer alive.
There is a great deal to be said
For being dead.

Edmund Clerihew Bentley,
*'Clive', (1905)* •1236

My soul, sit thou a patient
  looker-on;
Judge not the play before
  the play is done:
Her plot hath many changes;
  every day
Speaks a new scene; the
  last act crowns the play.

Francis Quarles, *Emblems (1635)
'Respice Finem'* •1238

Eternity's a terrible thought. I mean, where's it all going to end?

Tom Stoppard, *Rosencrantz and Guildenstern are Dead (1967)* •1239

I can't help it, the idea of the infinite torments me.

Alfred de Musset, *'L'Espoir en Dieu' (1838)* •1240

One dies only once, and it's for such a long time.

Molière, *Le Depit amoureux (1662)* •1241

I don't like to commit myself about heaven and hell — you see, I have friends in both places. Mark Twain •1242

This is no time for making new enemies.

Voltaire, on being asked to renounce the Devil on his deathbed. *Attrib.* •1243

What did it matter where you lay, once you were dead? In a dirty sump or in a marble tower on top of a high hill? You were dead, you were sleeping the big sleep, you were not bothered by things like that. Oil and water were the same as wind and air to you. You just slept the big sleep, not caring about the nastiness of how you died or where you fell.

American detective fiction writer Raymond Chandler, *The Big Sleep, 1939* •1244

Death has something to be
  said for it:
There's no need to get out
  of bed for it;
Wherever you may be,
They bring it to you, free.

Kingsley Amis, *'Delivery Guaranteed' (1979)* •1245

I lingered round them, under that benign
sky: watched the moths fluttering among
the heath and harebells; listened to the
soft wind breathing through the grass;
and wondered how anyone could ever
imagine unquiet slumbers for the
sleepers in that quiet earth.

Novelist Emily Brontë,
*Wuthering Heights, 1847,*
the closing lines •1248

The woman is perfected
Her dead
Body wears the smile
  of accomplishment

The opening lines to Sylvia Plath's last
poem, *'Edge',* written a week before her
suicide in 1963 •1246

My sole wish is to frustrate as utterly
as possible the post-mortem exploiter…
I have long thought of launching, by
a provision in my will, a curse no less
explicit than Shakespeare's own on
any such as try to move my bones.

Henry James, *letter 7 April 1914* •1249

Excuse My Dust.

Dorothy Parker, suggested epitaph for herself
•1247

I care not; a man can die but once; we owe God a death.

William Shakespeare, *Henry IV Part 2 (1597) III.ii* •1250

Only we die in earnest, that's no jest.

Walter Raleigh, *'On the Life of Man'* •1253

My name is Death: the last best friend am I

Robert Southey, *'The Lay of the Laureate' (1816)* •1251

This is the way the world ends Not with a bang but a whimper.

T.S. Eliot, *'The Hollow Men' (1925)* •1254

This fell sergeant, death, Is swift in his arrest.

William Shakespeare, *Hamlet (1601) V.ii* •1252

Most persons have died before they expire — died to all earthly longings, so that the last breath is only, as it were, the locking of the door of the already deserted mansion.

American physician and writer Oliver Wendell Holmes, *The Professor at the Breakfast Table, 1860* •1255

Just before she [Stein] died, she asked, 'What is the answer?' No answer came. She laughed and said, 'In that case, what is the question?' Then she died.

The final musings of Gertrude Stein, as told in Donald Sutherland, Gertrude Stein — A Biography of her Work (1951) •1256

Death has to be waiting at the end of the ride before you truly see the earth, and feel your heart, and love the world.

French playwright Jean Anouilh, The Lark (1955) •1257

Death be not proud, though some have called thee Mighty and dreadful, for thou art not so.

John Donne, Holy Sonnets (1609) •1258

The day which you fear as being the end of all things, is the birthday of your eternity.

Seneca •1259

The rest is silence.

William Shakespeare, Hamlet (1601) V.ii •1260

¶

# THE JOY
# OF WORDS

*A word, in a word, is complicated.*
**Steven Pinker,** *The Language Instinct (1994)* ·1261

*Words are, of course, the most powerful drug used by mankind.*

Rudyard Kipling, *speech, 14 February 1923* •1262

*Words are undervalued as a means of expression. Pictures tend to trivialise experience.*

Arthur Miller, *attrib., 1990* •1263

*Wordstruck is exactly what I was — and still am: crazy about the sound of words, the look of words, the taste of words, the feeling for words on the tongue and in the mind.*

Robert MacNeil, *Wordstruck (1989)* •1264

*When I feel inclined to read poetry I take down my Dictionary. The poetry of words is quite as beautiful as that of sentences. The author may arrange the gems effectively, but their shape and lustre have been given by the attrition of ages.*

Oliver Wendell Holmes, *The Autocrat of the Breakfast Table (1858)* •1265

*What a comfort a Dictionary is!*

Lewis Carroll, *Sylvie and Bruno Concluded (1893)* •1266

We talk about the tyranny of words, but we like to tyrannise over them too; we are fond of having a large superfluous establishment of words to wait upon us on great occasions; we think it looks important, and sounds well.

Charles Dickens, David Copperfield (1850) •1267

Words are like leaves; and where they most abound

Much fruit of sense beneath is rarely found.

Alexander Pope, An Essay on Criticism (1711) •1269

Continual eloquence is tedious.

Blaise Pascal, Pensées (1670) •1270

A definition is the enclosing a wilderness of ideas within a wall of words.

Samuel Butler (1835-1902), Notebooks (1912) •1268

I fear those big words, Stephen said, which make us so unhappy.

James Joyce, Ulysses (1922) •1271

*Et semel emissum volat irrevocabile verbum. — And once sent out a word takes wing beyond recall.*

Horace, *Epistles* •1272

*Oaths are but words, and words but wind.*

Samuel Butler, *Hudibras pt.2 (1664)* •1273

*Words are chameleons, which reflect the colour of their environment.*

Learned Hand, in *Commissioner v. National Carbide Corp. (1948)* •1274

*When I cannot see words curling like rings of smoke round me I am in darkness — I am nothing.*

Virginia Woolf, *The Waves (1931)* •1275

*The limits of my language mean the limits of my world.*

Ludwig Wittgenstein, *Tractatus Logico Philosophicus (1922)* •1276

*The unconscious is structured like a language.*

Jacques Lacan, *Escrits (1966)* •1277

*He gave man speech, and speech created thought,*

*Which is the measure of the universe.*

Percy Bysshe Shelley, *Prometheus Unbound (1820)* •1280

*Language can… be compared with a sheet of paper: thought is the front and sound the back; one cannot cut the front without cutting the back at the same time.*

Ferdinand de Saussure, *Course in General Linguistics (1916)* •1278

# Language is the dress of thought.

Samuel Johnson, *Lives of the English Poets (1779-81)* •1281

*An irony is a nipping jest, or a speech that hath the honey of pleasantness in its mouth, and a sting of rebuke in its tail.*

Edward Reyner, *Rules for the Government of the Tongue (1656)* •1279

*She understood, as women do more easily than men, that the declared meaning of a spoken sentence is only its overcoat, and the real meaning lies underneath its scarves and buttons.*

Peter Carey, *Oscar and Lucinda (1989)* •1282

He makes language as physical as a bruise.

John Carey on Ted Hughes; *Sunday Times 9 December 1979* •1283

Slang is language that rolls up its sleeves, spits on its hands and goes to work.

Carl Sandburg, in *New York Times 13 February 1959* •1286

Good heavens! For more than forty years I have been speaking prose without knowing it.

Molière, *Le Bourgeois Gentilhomme (1671)* •1284

Slang is, at least, vigorous and apt. Probably most of our vital words were once slang.

John Galsworthy, in his presidential address to the English Association in 1924; *Castles in Spain and Other Screeds (1927)* •1285

Remember that you are a human being with a soul and the divine gift of articulate speech; that your native language is the language of Shakespeare and Milton and The Bible; and don't sit there crooning like a bilious pigeon.

George Bernard Shaw, *Pygmalion (1916)* •1287

*Correct English is the slang of prigs who write history and essays. And the strongest slang of all is the slang of poets.*

George Eliot, *Middlemarch (1871-2)* •1288

*Stylists used to revere 'pure' English, but in reality English is about as pure as a factory effluent, and has displayed its mongrel toughness over the centuries by cannibalizing a picturesque array of foreign tongues from Greek to Polynesian.*

John Carey, in *Sunday Times 27 January 1985* •1289

*So now they have made our English tongue a gallimaufry or hodgepodge of all other speeches.*

Edmund Spenser, *The Shepheard's Calendar (1579)* •1290

*They spell it Vinci and pronounce it Vinchy; foreigners always spell better than they pronounce.*

Mark Twain, *The Innocents Abroad (1869)* •1291

*Humour is the first of the gifts to perish in a foreign tongue.*

Virginia Woolf, *The Common Reader (1st series, 1925) 'On Not Knowing Greek'* •1292

To speak English, one must place the tongue between the teeth, and I have lost my teeth.

Voltaire, to James Boswell, 24 December 1764; in Pottle (ed.) Boswell on the Grand Tour (1953) •1293

Grammer, the ground of al.

William Langland, c.1330-c.1400, The Vision of Piers Plowman •1296

[The] collective unconscious of the race is the OED.

James Merrill, in American Poetry Review, September/October 1979 'On James Merrill' •1294

In my view, the greatest achievement of these islands was not arrived at by an individual, and not imagined by a single genius, but created, honed and sustained by millions over the centuries: the English language.

Melvyn Bragg, in Observer 24 November 2002 •1295

The notion 'grammatical' cannot be identified with 'meaningful' or 'significant' in any semantic sense. Sentences (1) and (2) are equally nonsensical, but... only the former is grammatical.
(1) Colourless green ideas sleep furiously.
(2) Furiously sleep ideas green colourless.

Noam Chomsky, Syntactic Structures (1957) •1297

*My mother pointed out... that one could not say 'a green great dragon', but had to say 'a great green dragon.' I wondered why, and still do.*

J.R.R. Tolkein of his first forays into storywriting, aged seven; *letter to W.H. Auden, 7 June 1955* •1298

*They've a temper, some of them — particularly verbs: they're the proudest — adjectives you can do anything with, but not verbs — however, I can manage the whole lot of them!*

Lewis Carroll, *Through the Looking-Glass (1872)* •1299

*Would you convey my compliments to the purist who reads your proofs and tell him or her that I write in a sort of broken-down patois which is something like the way a Swiss waiter talks, and that when I split an infinitive, God damn it, I split it so it will stay split.*

Raymond Chandler, *letter to Edward Weeks, 18 January 1947* •1300

*The failure of English masters, at all the schools I attended, to give me any comprehension of the purpose of punctuation is splendidly evident in that story.*

Angus Wilson, regarding his first short story, *'Raspberry Jam' (1946);* in *The Wild Garden (1963)* •1301

Punctuation ought to be exact. Under ordinary circumstances, it is as hard for me to alter punctuation as to alter words, though I will admit that at times I am heady and irresponsible.

**Marianne Moore,** *letter to Ezra Pound, 19 January 1919* •1302

My spelling is Wobbly. It's good spelling but it Wobbles, and the letters get in the wrong places.

**A.A. Milne,** *Winnie-the-Pooh (1926)* •1304

Cut out all those exlamation marks. An exclamation mark is like laughing at your own joke.

**F. Scott Fitzgerald, in** *Beloved Infidel (1959)* •1303

The cure for mixed metaphors is for the patient to be obliged to draw a picture of the result. **Bernard Levin** •1305

*Whenever the literary German dives into a sentence, that is the last you are going to see of him till he emerges on the other side of the Atlantic with his verb in his mouth.*

Mark Twain, *A Connecticut Yankee in King Arthur's Court, 1889.* •1306

*I once heard a Californian student in Heidelberg say, in one of his calmest moods, that he would rather decline two drinks than one German adjective.*

Mark Twain, *A Tramp Abroad (1880)* •1308

*Waiting for the German verb is surely the ultimate thrill.* Flann O'Brien, Irish novelist and journalist. •1307

*Cast iron rules will not answer... what is one man's colon is another man's comma.*

Mark Twain, in *Charles Neider (ed.) Life as I Find It (1961)* •1309

I will not go down
to posterity talking
bad grammar.

Benjamin Disreali, while correcting proofs
of his final parliamentary speech; in *Robert
Blake, Disreali (1966)* •1310

This is the sort
of English up
with which I
will not put.

Winston Churchill, in *Ernest Gowers,
Plain Words (1948)* •1311

¶

*It is a good thing for an uneducated man to read books of quotations.*

Winston Churchill, *My Early Life* •1314

*Next to being witty yourself, the best thing is to quote another's wit.*

Christian N. Bovee, American lawyer and author •1312

*The nicest thing about quotes is that they give us a nodding acquaintance with the originator which is often socially impressive.*

Actor Kenneth Williams, in the preface to *Acid Depths, 1980* •1315

*A proverb is one man's wit and all men's wisdom.*

Lord John Russell, in *R.J. Mackintosh, Sir James Mackintosh (1835)* •1313

*Do you know, I pick up favourite
quotations, and store them in my
mind as ready armour, offensive or
defensive, amid the struggle of this
turbulent existence.*

Scottish poet Robert Burns, in a *letter
to Mrs Dunlop, 6 December, 1792* •1316

*I often quote myself — it adds
spice to my conversation.*

Irish playwright and critic
George Bernard Shaw •1319

# *I quote others only the better to express myself.*

French essayist Michel do Montaigne,
*Essays, Book 1, Chapter 26, 1580* •1317

*It would be nice if sometimes the kind
things I say were considered worthy of
quotation. It isn't difficult, you know,
to be witty or amusing when one has
something to say that is destructive, but
damned hard to be clever and quotable
when you are singing someone's praises.*

Noël Coward, in *William Marchant,
The Pleasure of His Company (1981)* •1318

*Those who cannot miss
an opportunity of saying
a good thing... are not
to be trusted with the
management of any
great question.*

William Hazlitt,
*Characteristics (1823)* •1320

*Pretentious quotations being the surest road to tedium.*

H.W. Fowler and F.G. Fowler, *The King's English (1906)* •1321

*Misquotation is, in fact, the pride and priviledge of the learned. A widely-read man never quotes accurately, for the rather obvious reason that he has read too widely.*

Hesketh Pearson, *Common Misquotations (1934)* •1323

*If I had a good quote, I'd be wearing it.*

American singer and song writer Bob Dylan in reply to a French journalist who asked for 'a good quote', quoted in *The Times, July 1981.* •1322

*What a good thing Adam had. When he said a good thing he knew nobody had said it before.*

Mark Twain, *Notebooks (1935)* •1324

**Oscar Wilde:** *How I wish I had said that.*
**Whistler:** *You will, Oscar, you will.*

James McNeill Whistler, in *R. Ellman, Oscar Wilde (1987)* •1325

**Polonius:** *What do you read, my lord?*
**Hamlet:** *Words, words, words.*

William Shakespeare, *Hamlet (1601) II.ii* •1326

No one means all he says, and yet very few say all they mean, for words are slippery and thought is viscous.

Henry Brooks Adams, *The Education of Henry Adams (1907)* •1327

'When I use a word,' Humpty Dumpty said in a rather scornful tone, 'it means just what I choose it to mean — neither more nor less.'

Lewis Carroll, *Through the Looking-Glass (1872)* •1328

Then you should say what you mean,' the March Hare went on. 'I do,' Alice hastily replied; 'at least - at least I mean what I say — that's the same thing, you know.' 'Not the same thing a bit!' said the Hatter. 'Why, you might just as well say that I see what I eat is the same thing as I eat what I see!'

Lewis Carroll, *Alice's Adventures in Wonderland (1865)* •1329

'Contrariwise,' continued Tweedledee, 'if it was so, it might be; and if it were so, it would be: but as it isn't, it ain't. That's logic.

Lewis Carroll, *Through the Looking-Glass (1872)* •1330

The trouble with words is that you never know whose mouths they've been in. Dennis Potter •1331

The word 'good' has many meanings. For example, if a man were to shoot his grandmother at a range of 500 yards, I should call him a good shot, but not necessarily a good man.

G.K. Chesterton •1332

I always have a quotation for everything — it saves original thinking.

Detective fiction writer Dorothy L Sayers, in *Have His Carcase (1932)* •1333

Epigram and truth are rarely commensurate. Truth has to be somewhat chiselled, as it were, before it will fit into an epigram.

Joseph Farrell, *Lectures of a Certain Professor.* •1334

John Wesley's conversation is good, but he is never at leisure. He is always obliged to go at a certain hour. This is very disagreeable to a man who loves to fold his legs and have out his talk, as I do.

Samuel Johnson, in *Boswell's Life of Samuel Johnson (1791) — 25 March 1776* •1335

*Circumlocution, n. A literary trick whereby the writer who has nothing to say breaks it gently to the reader.*

Ambrose Bierce, *The Devil's Dictionary (1911)* •1336

*It was the look which caused her to be known in native bearer and half-caste circles as 'Mogi-Mgumbi', which may be loosely translated as She On Who It Is Unsafe To Try Any Oompus Boompus.*

P.G. Wodehouse, *Money in the Bank, 1946* •1337

*If nobody ever said anything unless he knew what he was talking about, a ghastly hush would descend upon the earth.*

A.P. Herbert, English writer and humorist •1338

*If I reprehend anything in this world, it is the use of my oracular tongue, and a nice derangement of epitaphs!* Richard Brinsley Sheridan, *The Rivals (1775) III.iii* •1339

# *He is the very pineapple of politeness!*

*The Rivals, III.iii* •1340

*No caparisons, Miss, if you please! — Caparisons don't become a young woman.*

The Rivals, *IV.ii* •1341

*Comparisons are odious.*

William Shakespeare, *Much Ado About Nothing (1598-9) III.v* •1342

*The conclusion of your syllogism, I said lightly, is fallacious, being based upon licenced premises.*

Flann O'Brien, *At Swin-Two-Birds (1939)* •1343

¶

*True wit is Nature to advantage dressed,*

*What oft was thought, but ne'er so well expressed.*

Alexander Pope, *An Essay on Criticism (1711)* •1344

## To become a great writer, whatever you do — avoid piles.

T.S. Eliot •1345

*It is always the best policy to speak the truth — unless, of course, you are an exceptionally good liar.*

Jerome K. Jerome, in *The Idler, February 1892* •1346

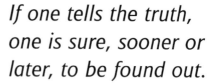

## If one tells the truth, one is sure, sooner or later, to be found out.

Oscar Wilde, *'Phrases and Philosophies for the use of the Young', 1894* •1347

**Cecil Graham:** *What is a cynic?*
**Lord Darlington:** *A man who knows the price of everything and the value of nothing.*

Oscar Wilde, *Lady Windermere's Fan, 1892.* •1348

## Wit is... the eloquence of indifference.

William Hazlitt, *Lectures on English Comic Writers (1818)* •1349

# Never trust a writer who uses his initials.

A.A. Gill •1350

Virginia Woolf subscribed to the theory that the pen was mightier than the sword; and I once saw the mighty Evelyn Waugh reel under a savage blow from her Parker 51.

Alan Bennett, *Forty Years On (1969)* •1351

Do not unto others as you would that they should do unto you. Their tastes may not be the same.

George Bernard Shaw, *Man and Superman, 'Maxims for Revolutionists: The Golden Rule' (1903)* •1352

I always pass on good advice. It is the only thing to do with it. It is never of any use to oneself.

Oscar Wilde, *An Ideal Husband (1895)* •1353

There is only one thing in the world worse than being talked about, and that is not being talked about.

Oscar Wilde, *The Picture of Dorian Gray, 1891* •1354

If, with the literate, I am impelled to try an epigram, I never asked to take the credit; we all assume that Oscar said it.

Dorothy Parker, *'Oscar Wilde', Sunset Gun, 1928* •1355

If you steal from one author, it's plagiarism; if you steal from many it's research.

Wilson Mizner, American playwright •1356

How come there's no other name for a thesaurus?

Wright Stevens •1362

When the wine is in, the wit is out.

Thomas Becon, *Catechism (1560)* •1357

You beat your pate, and fancy wit will come:

Knock as you please, there's nobody at home.

Alexander Pope, *'Epigram: You beat your pate' (1732)* •1358

Mark my words, when a society has to resort to a lavatory for its humour, the writing is on the wall.

Alan Bennett, *Forty Years On (1969)* •1360

*Nominations to find Britain's favourite poem include 'The Rhubarb of O'Mark I am'.*

Dennis O'Driscoll ·1361

*Oh, do let me go on. I want to see how it ends.*

Oscar Wilde, having been stopped midway through translating a passage from the Greek version of the New Testament in his viva at Oxford; in *James Sutherland (ed.), The Oxford Book of Literary Anecdotes* ·1359

¶

# THANKS TO

Arana, Marie (ed.),
*The Writing Life: Collection from Washington Post Book World (2003)*
(New York: PublicAffairs, 2003)

Kemp, Peter (ed.),
*The Oxford Dictionary of Literary Quotations*
(Oxford: Oxford University Press, 1997)

Knowles, Elizabeth (ed.),
*The Oxford Dictionary of Phrase, Saying and Quotation*
(Oxford: Oxford University Press, 1997)

Plimpton, George (ed.),
*The Writer's Chapbook*
(New York: Viking, 1989)

Plimpton, George (ed.),
*Writer's At Work: The Paris Review Interviews* (fourth series)
(London: Secker & Warburg, 1977)

Plimpton, George (ed.),
*Writer's At Work: The Paris Review Interviews* (seventh series)
(Harmondsworth: Penguin, 1988)

*Writers on Writing: Collected Essays from The New York Times*
(New York: Times Books, 2001)

*The Times Book of Quotations*
(Glasgow: Times Books, 2000)

Andrews, Robert (ed.),
*The New Penguin Dictionary of Modern Quotations*
(London: Penguin, 2003)

Bartlett, John (compiler),
*Bartlett's Shakespeare Quotations*
(New York: Little Brown & Co, 2005)

Bradfield, Bill (ed.),
*The Book of Ancient Wisdom*
(New York: Dover Publications, 2005)

Underwood, Lamar (ed.),
*The Quotable Writer*
(Guildford, CT: Lyons Press, 2004)

Magnusson, Magnus,
*Keeping My Words: An Anthology from Cradle to Grave*
(London: Hodder & Stoughton, 2005)

Metcalf, Fred (ed.),
*The Penguin Dictionary of Humorous Quotations* (2nd ed.)
(London: Penguin, 2002)

*The Literary Companion*
(London: Robson Books, 2004)

Leach, Maria (compiler),
*The Wicked Wit of Oscar Wilde*
(London: Michael O'Mara Books, 2000)

Enright, Dominique (compiler)
*The Wicked Wit of Jane Austen*
(London: Michael O'Mara Books, 2002)

Sherrin, Ned (ed.),
*The Oxford Dictionary of Humorous Quotations*
(Oxford: Oxford University Press, 2005)

*H. James*

P. G. Wodehouse

Voltaire

Henry D. Thoreau